09/07

DATE DUE FOR RETURN

FW

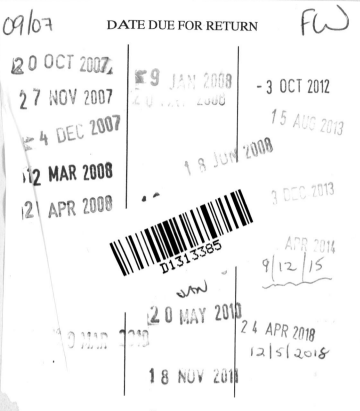

D1313385

Renewals
www.liverpool.gov.uk/libraries
0151 233 3000

R.267

The Last Executioner

Memoirs of Thailand's
Last Prison Executioner

by Chavoret Jaruboon

with Nicola Pierce

MAVERICK HOUSE PUBLISHERS.

Published by Maverick House, Main Street, Dunshaughlin, Co. Meath, Ireland.
Maverick House SE Asia, 440 Sukhumvit Road, Washington Square, Klongton, Klongtoey, Bangkok 10110, Thailand.

www.maverickhouse.com
email: info@maverickhouse.com

ISBN 1-905379-26-9
978-1-905379-26-2

Copyright for text © 2006 Chavoret Jaruboon
Copyright for typesetting, editing, layout, design © Maverick House Ltd
All images © Author's private collection

Printed and bound by Norhaven

5 4 3 2 1

The paper used in this book comes from wood pulp of managed forests. For every tree felled at least one tree is planted, thereby renewing natural resources.

A CIP catalogue record for this book is available from the British Library.

ACKNOWLEDGEMENTS

The book you're reading right now is the result of great support from my family and the good people around me. I'm very fortunate to have met so many good people in my life.

I found it hard, when I first started, to recollect my life prior to my job at the prison, and the executions in details, and there are too many stories to tell. Luckily, I have journals, paperwork and reports that help remind me of what happened.

I guess I inherit the passion to teach people from my father, and I am glad of that.

Thanks to my friend Susan Aldous. Thanks to all at Maverick House Publishers; especially to Pornchai Sereemongkonpol and John Mooney for your great contribution in making my dream come true. Many thanks also to Nicola Pierce.

Thank YOU for choosing this book and reading it. I hope this book could teach you a thing or two about life and please don't be tempted to make a wrong choice and end up in Bang Kwang, or any prison.

I would like to take the last paragraph to ask for forgiveness from the victims and convicts whom I mentioned in this book. May they all rest in peace and if there is any good to come out of this book, I would like to dedicate it to them.

DEDICATION

To my father and teacher Chum, the best father a son could ask for. Thanks for sending me to Catholic school. Thanks for the guitar you bought me. I guess I inherit the passion to teach people from you because I am now invited to speak to students in schools and universities about crimes, so I am sort of a teacher too. I hope you are proud of me.

PROLOGUE

23 November 1984.

There were three that day; I shot two.

The day before, I had celebrated my 36th birthday, but that day I had to prepare myself to kill a man for the first time. Ten years of experience had brought me to this defining moment. I had worked my way up from handling the prisoner, to adjusting and aiming the gun used to kill the condemned, and now I had been promoted to the most prominent position of all. I was the executioner.

The prisoners were very calm. You never know how they will react when it is their turn. When I used to escort the men from their cells to their death, I could almost smell the relief of those spared for another day. By the time I came to take them, the doomed convict would have already given away his stuff to the other inmates; all that was left to do was say his goodbyes. I was told later that Samran, one of the inmates waiting to die, kept reassuring his friends and maybe himself by chanting, 'It's my time bro, it's my time'.

The convicts followed the guards out of the wing, eyes to the ground. Nobody spoke. What was there to say? You would not insult a 'dead man walking' by asking him again if he was really guilty—it was too late anyway for a declaration of innocence. Besides, they were guilty. We knew that and they knew that. Two of them had achieved notoriety with their gang of thieving murderers. The third one worked solo, with the same results. Each man was getting the punishment he had earned for himself, through his own actions.

I was surprised to discover that I was a little nervous. I was still feeling fresh from my nap and shower I'd had that day. You see, I wanted to look my best; it would help me concentrate. I had gotten my wife Tew to iron my second uniform. She was surprised to see me home so early that day, and even more surprised to be told that I was returning to work for an evening shift. I would tell her later—maybe.

After ten years of playing supporting roles in this execution process I was finally taking the lead part.

My one desire was that they would die immediately, without pain. I had hand-picked the fifteen bullets myself. I did not expect to use them all, but I had witnessed enough errors over the years to persuade me to be fully prepared, just in case. It had to be a perfect, clean shot. There would be a lot of blood when we were finished.

I aimed the HK MP5 at the target and suddenly realised that I had forgotten to cock the gun. Trying to hide my panic I kept my face expressionless, ignoring the rest of the execution team and the officials. All eyes were on me as I carefully cocked the gun and took my aim again. The audience waited, in mute anticipation. Lhee, the condemned, was the only one unaware of my embarrassment.

I felt like I was on stage once more, dressed like Elvis Presley, and playing my guitar for the American soldiers like I had done in my younger days. Except now I was going to take a life. When people ask me if I am ever afraid of being haunted by dead convicts, I tell them I am more afraid of my wife.

My name is Chavoret Jaruboon and I am a legend. I am the last person in Thailand to execute criminals with a gun. I have shot 55 men and women, and this is my story.

CHAPTER 1

I was born on 22 November 1948, in Watchira Hospital, around the Sri Yan area of Bangkok. Bangkok, the City of Angels which translates as Krung Thep, is the largest city in Thailand with a population today of about 6 million. A long time ago it had a much longer name—Krungthep mahanakhon amonratanakosin mahintara ayuthaya mahadilok popnopparat ratchathani burirom udomratchaniwet mahasathan amonpiman avatansathit sakkathattiya witsanukamprasit. Fortunately you don't have to write that on an envelope now. If you did, there would be no room for the stamp.

My mother was Vilai Cholpinthu, an Islamic woman and daughter of Laung (a title granted by the Royal family) Navavijidshoonrabanthu, who was an engineer for the Royal battleship. She was my father's third wife. When his first wife died he married again. Then he separated from his second wife to marry my mother. It seems that he was just unlucky in the women he chose, although I do think he truly loved his first wife. In the olden days men used to collect wives and house them with their children under one roof. The more dependants you had the more of a man you were. The downside of this was that it could lead to battles of epic proportions that no man had any business involving himself in. After nearly 40 years of marriage, personally, I think one wife is enough for any man!

Thankfully, there was never any fighting in our house but, all the same, when I was four or five years old my parents divorced, leaving my father to raise me and my older brother Oud. It is strange but even today I don't know what happened between them. Nothing was explained to me at the time because I was just a child, and then, as I got older, it never came up as a topic with my father. Maybe he thought it was none of my business. His motto was, 'Silent tongue means wise heart,' and he was always a quiet man anyway.

In hindsight I imagine that there could have been an issue about religious differences with my mother's family since my father was a Buddhist. I don't remember much about my mother's family. I may have just met them once or twice. I do remember thinking though that it was quite an achievement for her father, who was an ordinary man, to become a high-ranking officer in the Navy.

My mother would visit me from time to time but we were never that close. I much preferred Chum Jaruboon, my father. His people were from Banggruay in Nonthaburi. He was one of three kids. By the time his mother passed away there was only himself and his younger sister left. Typically of my father, he gave his entire inheritance to his little sister because he thought that he should be able to support himself, being a proud man. He was never a wealthy man and had no great financial acumen. Shortly before I was born, he had sold some property that he owned and used the money to open up a taxi business. Unfortunately the business never took off and he was forced to shut it down.

He was already on the wrong side of 50 by the time I came along but I could talk to him about anything, except the time that I got beaten up by the school bully. I kept that to myself because it would have upset him too much. He was a teacher, and I decided that I wanted to be one too—it was cool to see his students bowing to him. Education was very important to him and he made it important for me too.

In many ways, he was ahead of his time. He taught art, drama and was also a photographer. I learned English by listening to his Frank Sinatra and Eddie Williams records. Unlike my friends' fathers he didn't push me to join the army and believed in letting me decide for myself what I would do with my life. He probably spoilt me a little, to compensate for the divorce. I always had more toys than my friends. When it came to pocket money he gave me more than I deserved. He used to give me money every day but then he decided that I should learn to save, so he paid me a weekly rate on a Monday morning. However, when I ran through my money by Thursday I knew he was good for extra baht to keep me going until the 'official' pay day. He wasn't too strict either, and trusted me, so it wasn't a problem when I wanted to stay in town with my friends after school to eat noodles and window shop. He understood that I had a private life away from home and school.

He also wanted to encourage my interest in music and sent me to a Catholic school; Saint Joan of Arc. Most of the kids went to the Thai school, so I felt very privileged. I enjoyed school and was frequently top of the class. I suppose you could say that I was the teacher's pet, but I also got on well with my class mates. I never got involved in fights and understood from a young age that some kids felt they had to act tough in order to be accepted by their peers. But that wasn't for me. I wasn't afraid of being unpopular with certain people.

One day I gave Chan, my teacher, a hard time. I'm afraid that, in my youth, I could be prone to showing off. I argued with her, in front of the whole class, over the spelling of Wednesday, which I pronounced Wed-nes-day. Her face got redder and redder as I obstinately argued my case for my version—the correct one. I thought she would surely tell me to get out of the room; I would have if I was her. Instead she scowled and said, 'Fine! If you don't believe me, your teacher, then go learn some place else.' Well, I was absolutely offended. Being sure to maintain my boyish dignity, I picked up my bag and books and, without a second glance at that unreasonable woman, I walked out of the room with my nose in the air. She probably thought that I would stand outside the door, as was the usual procedure, but I was so angry I just kept walking, down the corridor, out of the door, and down the street. I was rather smug when I heard later that she had been really worried and looked everywhere for me—even taking my brother out of his class to help her.

Unfortunately my school days weren't all like this. I remember being heartily laughed at by my peers when I was confronted by another teacher, Pao, about the dirty dead skin behind my ears. Maybe the pipes were broken at home, or maybe I put up too good a fight over bathing for a while, but Pao pounced on me during a class inspection and loudly asked if I was storing up the dead skin to eat. I was mortified and timidly replied, 'No eat', speaking so softly that everyone just heard me say 'eat'. I wasn't allowed to forget that for quite a long time. And if I was really unlucky one of the kids might remind everyone else of my shitting my pants in grade two; I had diarrhoea and kept having to ask the teacher for permission to go to the toilet. In exasperation she told me to stay where I was and let it all out. Perhaps she didn't believe me—but she certainly did ten minutes later when she had to replace my soiled trousers.

When I was in grade four I committed my one and only crime, which I feel safe to confess now. There were two Chinese boys in my class, Surasak and Kriengsak, and their father ran a printing business. On New Year's Eve they brought packs of greeting cards to school to present to all the students. I was fascinated by them;

they were all brightly coloured, some of them were of movie stars, some had beautiful rural landscapes and some of them were of the Royal family. Fortunately, for me, our classmates didn't seem that bothered with them. The two boys had carefully placed one greeting card on each desk, making sure that everyone got one. Some were allowed to fall to the floor and most didn't command much attention after an initial glance. I decided that the cards were wasted on these heathens, and at the first opportunity I took them; all of them. I worried for a couple of weeks that I would end up in jail, and as I've said I never did anything like that again, but at least I got to gaze at those beautiful pictures whenever I wanted to.

***

I suppose I was a good child but I didn't have a sheltered upbringing at Soi 1, my father's house. We lived between the wealthy and the poor, high-ranking officials and junkies, at Sri Yan junction. I could see the slum, brothel and porn theatres at one end of the Soi, which means street, while at the other end were the big houses and gardens of the judges, colonels and president of the Privy Council. All the prominent men had their own private car and chauffeur, a far cry from the prostitutes and their clientele. You could see the brothel from our house; it was nothing more than a shack built on marshy ground. I think I must be one of the few Thai men who has never gone to a brothel— my father always warned me about how dirty they are. I would peer through the entrance, from a safe distance, fascinated by the stained walls and utter degradation. It was also an opium house and there were always Chinese addicts hanging around. Opium was still legal then and my father would worry about me, but I was never tempted to try drugs of any kind. There was always a tension between the rich and poor, and evening battles between the different mobsters were a regular occurrence. My father would constantly warn me against losing sight of who I was, saying, 'Don't be phlegm or people will look down on you.'

I left Saint Joan of Arc in 1958, and started my fifth grade at Wat Rachathiwas School, under the tutelage of Pikul Saengthong. Looking at my report cards today I am reminded that I was quite a good student. I had a high average percentage and my best subject was English, with Mathematics being my weakest. My aptitude for English could probably be explained by the focus on the subject at my previous school. In Thailand, private schools started to teach English almost immediately, while the public school would only start teaching it in grade 5. It was no wonder then that I was way ahead of my less privileged class mates. No doubt I exploited my superiority over them. Showing off was my only motivation to do well, and I was always in the top ten.

There was an emphasis on sport at this school. Prasit Ampanseang, a Thai boxing judge was my gym teacher. However, sport was one of a long list of things that I did not excel in. I did not enjoy the constant training or the possibility of getting hurt. The school was well-known, albeit locally, for its prowess in basketball and takraw. Sepak takraw is an ancient sport and is a mixture of soccer, volleyball, gymnastics and *kung fu*. It involves using a tremendous amount of energy to prevent a ball, the size of a grapefruit, from touching the ground. You can use any part of your body except your hands—a brilliant spectator sport, and I should know since I wasn't selected to play on the school team!

I kept a good average score throughout the years and grew up happy with my own learning. I was very much just like any other boy, and wanted the same things. I kept my head down and listened to my father and my teachers, for the most part, but kept a vague sense of moving on, not sure what exactly I wanted to do when I left.

***

During the summer break I got my first job. A friend of my brother asked me to work as a doorman at a bar in Patpong. The pay was a paltry 300 baht a month but at least I got to practice my English. I perfected sentences like, 'Good evening sir,' 'What can I do for you?' and, 'Bye bye sir.' When I gained a bit more confidence, I would start conversations about music. The owner of the bar was a pregnant woman called Deang. I didn't like her or her bar which never did much business. I waited until I received my pay packet and then quietly quit, in that I didn't inform her—I just never went back. I reasoned that there must be a more pleasant way of making money. Back home I proudly showed off my first wages to my father and immediately used them to buy a pair of fashionable shoes. I was very into my clothes and liked to look as well as I, or my father, could afford.

CHAPTER 2

My world was transformed in 1966 when I got my first guitar. My father bought two second-hand guitars; one for me and one for my friend. I taught myself to play, with a little help from my friends, in particular my friend Nui. I hadn't harboured any particular ambition towards becoming a musician, but then again I was one of those kids who just muddled through from one day to the next, without focus or plan. I certainly wasn't a natural; I merely spent many, many weeks with a throbbing thumb, strumming away badly. My father also made me a 15 watt amplifier which I managed to lose at a fair. Instead of being angry with me he went out to sell ornaments that he collected, from the horns of buffalo, and a wild pig's head so that he could make me another one. That was the type of man he was.

After a lot of practice, I formed a band with my friends and we called ourselves Victory. We played our first gig on Children's Day, at the invitation of a teacher. This holiday takes place in January, on the second Saturday. Schools organize special activities, and there are special TV programmes laid on for kids that day, plus they can ride the buses and go into the theme parks for free. We couldn't get on to the stage fast enough. There was no payment, but I loved the girls screaming at us.

Our fourth gig at a private party finally provided us with a wage—30 baht each—a tiny amount that I was very proud of. Meanwhile, my friend's band, Mitra, was competing at Suan Amporn near Suan Dusit Palace, which had a rotating stage that I thought was very cool. As usual my father was very supportive of my new hobby and would give me money so that I could dress like my heroes Elvis Presley and Cliff Richard, an opportunity I took up quickly.

My all-time hero was, and still is today, the 'King'. I loved all his songs and even his movies: *Loving You, Blue Hawaii, Jailhouse Rock* and *Fun In Acapulco*. As soon as I saw him I went out and bought myself a denim shirt and jeans and spent hours in front of the mirror trying to move my legs and hips like him. In Thailand we referred to his dancing as being like 'a worm in burning ash', and I did my best to replicate him on stage.

The popular local bands at the time were The Charming Boys, White House and F Five. They were heavily influenced by The Shadows, who were huge in Thailand. Mitra came seventh in the national music competition and were doing very well for themselves so I was delighted when they asked me to replace their bassist. I had applied to go to a vocational school in Nonthaburi, after deciding to study manufacturing mechanics, but had failed the all-important examination. In my defence there was extremely stiff competition for the college places, and yes I admit to not trying too hard for the entrance exam—maybe I knew I was meant for something else.

Mitra is short for Mitranon, the band manager's name. He came from Thonburi and his two sons played guitar and drums in the band. My friend, Daeng played base guitar and sang, and I played chord guitar. We were booked to play at the Corsair restaurant-bar in Ubolratchathani. Restaurant owners hired the top three bands in Bangkok, and would provide travel expenses and accommodation up front. I was so excited that I couldn't sleep on the 12 hour train journey from Bangkok to Ubolratchathani. We were collected at the station to be brought into the city centre. I remember being glad to see the Chalermsin movie theatre and planning to spend a lot of time there. It was all so exciting.

It took just 15 minutes to reach Corsair, which was a typical highway restaurant-bar. There was no roof over the stage, and the customers had their pick of deck-chairs or dining chairs with cushions. The waitresses wore pink and the grey stage was bathed in garish red, green and yellow lighting when we played. Only Thai beer and liquor was served to the mostly soldier clientele. There was big money to be made. I got 100 baht per night which was a huge amount to me. In those days a decent meal cost 50 satang and a tram ticket cost 25 satang, so I was loaded. The morning after the first gig I spent 45 baht on a proper tailor-made shirt, and looked and felt like a star.

We played to the American soldiers who arrived in Thailand, looking to have a fun time away from the war in Vietnam. Their camps were near by, and they would swarm to hear us play. We played a lot of Hank Williams, who was still the king of country music then, despite having died in mysterious circumstances back in 1953 at the tender age of 29. He has since deservedly become an icon of country music and rock 'n' roll. He was one of the initiators of the Honky Tonk style, and had a huge repertoire of songs for us to choose from, with stuff like, 'Your Cheatin' Heart' and 'I'll Never Get Out of This World Alive'. Daeng was a really good singer, we could work the crowd, and we always got a raucous reception. They would sometimes shout out requests, and one time when we complied for a soldier, he removed his cap and passed it around his buddies. The band received 1,000 baht each from this one tip—I will never forget that.

We stayed in rented accommodation near the bar. It was an old wooden house that we shared with the owner and her three kids. We all got along fine and I would frequently bring the kids to the cinema. We lived there for four months and then we moved to another house in the centre of town. Our new land-lady was a fat middle-aged woman called Patum. She was obsessed with the electricity bill. If we switched on an extra light she would moan about it for days. It didn't bother me because I was rich now. When I had first arrived my entire wardrobe consisted of two shirts, two pairs of pants and one old jacket that a friend had given me. Now I was the proud owner of several suits, and not only that, I was also able to send money back home.

The restaurant did great business with the soldiers, in drinks and women. There were a lot of women around; some were waitresses and some were prostitutes. They had to be good looking or else the owner would tell them to take a hike. The better looking a girl was, the more customers she attracted. I always pitied the hookers who worked for a commission based on the drinks they sold. They only had basic English, but usually it was all they needed. Towards the end of the night you would hear them almost challenge the Americans: 'You go with me tonight? Short time or all night?'

The bars really were a little seedy, and very lively. To be allowed to work in the bar, a woman had to have a doctor's letter stating that she was free from any venereal diseases. A soldier could hire a woman for the night, paying for her at the bar along with his drink. The owner would check that the girl was willing, which was something at least. She would nod her consent and a deal was struck. It was easy money for the women I suppose. Though perhaps I shouldn't put it like that because it must have been awful for them. They got paid in dollars which were usually sent back to their parents. If the farang was charged 300 baht she probably got 50 baht out of it, which was crap. She also wouldn't be paid straight away. The owners didn't want to lose a 'good' girl so they would only get paid maybe once a month. Also, if the owner waited a month to pay up then he might not have to pay at all if the girl was poached to work for another bar. Any girl who moved on could forget about trying to collect her commission owed.

I can't really say that most of the women were forced into prostitution; some actually did it out of love for their families. They wanted their parents to have the TV set like the next door neighbours' whose daughter bought them their set with her earnings from selling her body. It was just a job to them. They hadn't got the patience or money to go to college and get a degree, and career opportunities were few and far between for women anyway, so this was a short-term option. These women thought themselves to be quite independent and knew that they wouldn't be doing this forever.

There was also a strip show, but it wasn't X-rated like the shows in places like Patpong. Patpong used to be a lot different than it is today—I hear there are always a few disappointed tourists wandering around the town looking for something left behind from its 'glory days' of the 60s and 70s. Now, it seems a lot seedier, with far more explicit sex shows, but back then it was more of a white collar area. The girls would usually just remove their bras, while swinging their hips in time to a drumbeat, with a chorus of Americans shouting, 'Take it off. Take it off.' The men would shove dollar notes between the girls' breasts and urge them to go further—they just might remove their panties if they were tipped generously enough. Even so, if the girls did decide to treat the men, the lights would go off the second their knickers did.

Being a young man with more cash than I'd ever had before, it was only natural that I got acquainted with a lot of these women, the singers, the masseurs and the bar girls. I lost my virginity to a bar girl. I knew that these girls had been tested for VD and I was always careful to only sleep with clean girls. My father had already warned about this disease and its symptoms— you pee like a fountain and you might go blind. I wasn't like a typical customer with these girls. Some of them were close to me in age and we just flirted and dated like a regular teenage couple and eventually had sex. I was quiet and trustworthy. I was never very handsome but I was always generous and liked to give girls little presents. They knew I was from Bangkok. I dressed well compared to the locals and I had my own money, although I had no savings and lived from wage packet to wage packet. I stopped short of going to brothels thanks to my father's warning when I was younger, against the dirt and possible lurking germs in these places.

***

I had great fun with the Americans. They taught me how to curse with expressions like 'Fuck you' and 'Go to hell, goddamit'. It was probably different for us, a band from Bangkok. Everyone else—bar owners, girls and taxi drivers—just saw walking dollar signs, whereas we got a chance to befriend them. We had our own money and didn't need anything from them. Instead, we would buy them dinner and just hang out—drinking and dancing to the latest hits on the juke-box. I got to know some of them really well, including John who was a technician and loved nothing more than to drink, flirt and ride his motorbike. I learned to distinguish the grey uniform pilots (couriers) from the orange uniforms (fighters). In one of the American camps I remember there was a bell hanging over the bar. When you heard the bell it meant that your food and drink was on the house—a sort of 'welcome home' present for the fighter pilots. If you were empty-handed, you would be given a beer.

Bangkok was a little behind the times, musically. These guys introduced me to their favourite songs that were always completely new to me. There was a Pete Seeger song, 'Where Have All The Flowers Gone?' that was especially popular and a few instrumentals that were hits for the American band The Ventures, including the Hawaii Five-O theme. I would buy Thai beer like Singha or Meh Khong for them and they would buy me their foreign beer. They were supplied with coupons for duty free goods; each man was allowed six bottles of liquor and three cartons of cigarettes, which was ample for bartering. They were also able to get large appliances which they could either sell on to Thai shopkeepers or bring back to their rent-wives.

Commissioned officers rented out bungalows near the camp which they would furnish with a 'wife'. These women were different from the normal run-of-the-mill prostitutes, in that they would live with their man as if they were his wife. In fact some couples did actually marry and return to the US as proper man and wife. For the most part, however, the woman would be left behind with her 'red-headed' children when the 'husband' was summoned to Korea or the Philippines. I befriended quite a few of them; some of them were really quite pitiful. They got swallowed up by their circumstances and simply surrendered. Their Thai families would be quite disinterested in their unhappiness, only wanting them to send money as often as possible, instead of telling their daughters to walk away from this life of almost-prostitution.

The women I met felt trapped and abandoned, and were usually in dire need of money, either for aging parents or for their children's education. These children of mixed descent are like a new generation of Thai people today. Thai people like 'farang' children and some of them have made a career for themselves in the media. I think it is interesting that white women never date Thai men but white men have no qualms about dating Thai women.

Some rich Thai people made huge economic gains thanks to the Vietnam War. They would do their research and find out where the Americans planned to build their camps and military bases. Then they rushed out to buy the desired property, and made a killing in re-selling it to the American army.

***

It was a good time in my life, especially since I was a teenager, and seeing all that the entertainment business had to offer me, I decided to forget about school and concentrate on music instead. Besides, the money was too much to walk away from. My father never complained but I think he would have preferred me to continue on with my studies. I ended up staying with Mitra for a year, and got to see a few different places. When the Corsair got a new band, we got a booking with the Hawaii Bar, which then became the Miami Bar. This wasn't as busy as Corsair but I enjoyed it just as much.

One night I was completely taken by surprise when my father walked in. I spotted him immediately from the stage. During this time I kept in contact with my family through infrequent letters. It had been a while since I wrote, so my worried father jumped on the train and made the 12 hour journey to see me play and make sure I was alright. After the gig we went for something to eat.

He told me that he had paid a visit to the governor of Ubolratchathani, who had been a student of his. He first went looking for the governor at his home but he wasn't there so he went down to his office. He was dressed very casually for an official visit and was reminded of this by the frostiness of the governor's secretary who asked him for identification and instructed him to fill out a form. She told him that her boss was in an important meeting and she wasn't going to interrupt him. My father nodded agreeably and sat down to wait. The secretary was struck dumb when the governor appeared and cried out at the sight of his former teacher. He immediately embraced him and introduced him to his companions. He even asked him to talk at the teachers' seminar which he was opening the following day, which he did.

The next day, he was grinning from ear to ear when a black Mercedes-Benz arrived to pick him up and then drop him back to my place after the seminar. He stayed with me for five days and then headed back to Bangkok. It was great to see him, and I promised myself I would keep in touch a lot more.

Sadly my letters continued to be infrequent even after this visit. I should have written to him a lot more than I did. This remains one of my biggest regrets. It probably made his day when he did receive a note of some description from me. He had retired by then and just longed to keep up with my day to day routine. I always intended to write a letter to accompany the money I sent him, but to get to the Post Office I had to pass—or try to pass—by the theatre. More often than not I would end up sitting in a plush seat in front of the big screen, and then would have to dash to make the post and there would be no time to write anything. My heart clenches every time I read this letter:

Dear Pom (his nickname for me)

I got your money order son. Today is 21 February 1967 3.30pm. You've not sent me letter lately. I guess you don't have time for it or you don't know what to write. I too don't know what to write. However, I'm relieved now knowing you're OK. You decide for yourself what you should do and what you should not. I leave the decision up to you. You should write me one letter a week at least. Two would be better .

Hope you're happy there.

Sawasdee.

***

My favourite drinking hole was Noknoi nightclub. We would go there in the afternoon to partake in the Tea Dance. I don't know why it was called that since there was no dancing and certainly no tea—instead everyone was drinking beer or liquor. Noknoi was only one of two nightclubs in Ubolratchathani, the other was King Star. There were a few bars, and after they closed we would head to a 'coffee shop' for a last beer along with a plate of fried chicken. I had a leisurely life-style then. My typical day began at 10am approximately. We usually caught a movie about mid-day and then we would practice in the afternoons. As I say we got along fine with the American soldiers. We had a lot in common with them, and were close to them in age. I was also careful to get on with the local people, and chatted to the rickshaw drivers. Sometimes I would get a gig playing at Chaloemsin, just over the bridge from Ubolratchathani. Because I had money I could grab a taxi or rickshaw instead of taking the pink and white bus, but there was a problem with them at first as they didn't want our Thailand bank notes. Everyone wanted the American dollar.

It sounds crass to say that I enjoyed the Vietnam War, but I was a young man, whose day was spent listening to and playing music, drinking beer with my friends, without any real responsibility. I had plenty of money and could indulge my fondness for fashion and good clothes. I loved to dress well and no one knew that better than my father. If I ever needed proof of his love for me I need look no further than the fact he bought me a pair of made-to-order Jalernchai shoes. These shoes were all the rage at the time—well, among kids richer than me—and cost the equivalent of an average month's wage. Of course, the war would impinge on our fun when an American friend wouldn't make it back from the front—a brutal reminder that life could be very short indeed. I think what I liked about the Americans was that they treated everyone equally. Thai people judge you on how much money you have while the American just wants to know you can do the job. They would give someone a tool-box and let him prove that he could fix a motorbike. If he could, he had a job, regardless of who he was.

I was impressed by stars like Bob Hope, who would play two shows, one for the officers in their clubs and another for the NCO (non-commissioned officers) club. If the commissioned officers wanted to see the second show they would have to come in civilian clothes or else they would be booed. The men talked constantly about going home, and most of them did not seem certain about what they were fighting for. They could not get enough of that song '500 Miles Away From Home'. It was one of their most requested songs and they would all join in and sing about not having a shirt on their back or a penny to their name. Another popular tune was 'Leaving on a Jet Plane'. Again, it was all about going home.

One time I left Mitra at the urging of Toi, a friend from home. I got on a bus to join him in Lop Buri, a town north of Bangkok, to play bass guitar, but this arrangement barely lasted seven days. I didn't go out much and the pay wasn't good. However, as it was a lot nearer to Bangkok my father came out to see me again. The manager of Mitra rang him at home to ask if I would play with them again, this time in Udornthani, in the north-eastern region of Thailand. I did not have to think hard about my decision; I promptly apologised to Toi and wished him the best of luck, and left Lop Buri with my father. I caught another bus to Udornthani. I had never been there before but my father was told to tell me to go the Lotus bar, which was in front of the big US military camp. I worried that I wouldn't get off at the right stop, but once the bus dropped me off I found myself looking at Lotus, directly across from the bus-stop. I could hear music and sure enough Mitra were on stage when I went in. I relaxed with a cold beer until the band saw me and beckoned me to join them. The line-up had changed; there were two singers, a Chinese girl and a guy from Malaysia, and a saxophonist, Thep Sornvijit, the only name I remember now. We spent a week there, playing every night to the Americans, which meant a lot of drinking and partying. I loved it. I started to band-hop, like a freelance musician, which was a good excuse to travel and see different places.

***

Sometime in 1968 I arrived in Sattaheep, which is right on the coast of the Gulf of Thailand. There was an American camp here too; I think it was called Camp Vayama. I stayed for two months, playing at the Ponderosa restaurant-bar. The owner also owned the local bath house where I spent many a relaxing afternoon. I was joining another old pal, this time from Saint Joan of Arc, who played guitar in a group with two bad-tempered Chinese girls.

They looked comical onstage, standing side by side, because one was very fat and the other one was skinny. I didn't get a chance to get to know them very well as they left the band abruptly after a fight with one of the guitarists. However, I made a lot of other friends over the two months. I learned how to bowl and play cards, in that order. It's true what they say about gambling—when you win money, you want to play again to win more, and when you lose money, you want to play again to get it back. The money wasn't that great, though I was living cheaply enough, and my accommodation was just a small room provided by the bar. My meals were free, but not very appetising. I was caught up quite happily in my own life, barely registering the world outside my life of gigs, girls and gambling, but there were constant reminders that the world was still turning. At night I could hear the B52 planes taking off and then hear them return in the early hours of the morning, their deadly mission completed.

My father came to see me at Sattaheep. It was a surprise visit so it was lucky that I decided to bus into the city centre. I saw him, from the window, with Oud my older brother and Seena, my half-sister, from one of my father's previous marriages. They came to the Ponderosa to have dinner and watch me play. I hadn't seen my siblings in quite a while and I was delighted to catch up with them, and show off my musical talent and my many new friends.

When our gig ended with the Ponderosa I went home to Bangkok where I hung out with old friends and practised my guitar a lot. Then, a DJ I knew, Surachai Thomdirat, rang to ask me if I would go to play in Ta Khli, in the province of Nakhon Sawan, which is north-west of Bangkok, a few hours past Lop Buri. It was quite a large, busy city, very modernized compared to most places I had been. I jumped at the opportunity. The following day I left Bangkok on the 1pm train and arrived in Ta Khli four hours later. There was a big American camp there, so there were plenty of farangs on the streets and everyone was well dressed with plenty of style. There was also lots of traffic, buses, trucks as well as the more humble tricycles. To my delight there were plenty of bars and bath houses that lined both sides of the streets, and there were no less than two movie theatres, Chalermwattana and Sripornsawan, though they sadly lacked air-conditioning. There was also a large fresh food market with plenty of variety; I couldn't believe the many different types of food on offer. Up on the mountain in Ta Khli, the US Army Airforce Radar and Communication Site was clearly visible. This base was very strict compared to the others and the guards were really uptight about who could enter or leave the camp. I later found out that this was to do with the F111 which was supposed to be top secret, but obviously wasn't. The F111 was meant to be the absolutely most up to date war plane with the highest of high-tech equipment, and it was stationed there. Despite all this hoo-hah, however, I do know that not all of those fantastic planes made it back to the base.

I played in three different bars there over a period of six months. I was in a group that included another school friend of mine, Odd. Quite possibly he was the reason I got the job. The first bar we played at was the American Bar, run by a large Thai woman. She hired us for two months, and as was usual, provided us with accommodation, letting us have an old house behind the bar. It's a house that I will never forget. I moved my stuff into a room on the second floor while Odd bagged a room on the ground floor. After a couple of nights he began to complain that the house was haunted. I wasn't sure if I believed him or not but when his complaints got louder I decided to give him the benefit of the doubt and spend the night in his room—he wasn't making it up. I awoke at some stage in the night when my bed started to shake violently for no reason, and then, to my horror, I saw the outline of a woman sitting silently on a chair against the wall. I couldn't really see her face as she was staring down into her lap, but she had long dark hair. She never looked or spoke to me, which is a good thing because I had lost my tongue, and couldn't even scream. After a couple of seconds she vanished, and so did I, never to spend another night in that room.

We did very well in Ta Khli and proved very popular. We included acrobats and silly stunts as part of our act, and a lot of our songs were heavily laden with a great drum beat. I was now able to play bass guitar, which improved my confidence as a musician. Thailand's Elvis replaced us when we left for our next post, the Sorry About That Bar, where we played for three months. This was a big place that used to be a roller-skating rink, and was run by a kindly Chinese man, who was from my home town in Bangkok. The bar was in the centre of the hall so there was plenty of room for the popular floor shows. Odd left the band around this time and was replaced by Tui, a married man from Nonthaburi. We must have been decent enough because I remember someone recording us rehearsing one day. We also played at the Sripornsawan theatre, with other local bands, thanks to DJ Surachai, who had joined us by then, but the money wasn't great.

When our three months were up we got a booking at the Black Jack bar, but this turned out to be a very quick visit. The owner wasn't very prompt at paying us so our managers, Maitri and Tawil Mitranon, decided that we should move on to Udorn. We sneaked out in the dead of night, which is not something I'm necessarily proud of. So I was back in Udorn again the following afternoon. The bar that booked us, the Las Vegas, was still being renovated. It looked more like a nightclub, and had a big dance floor. We heard that a farang had been shot dead here, under a previous owner, which thrilled us a little.

Things started off well. We all shared a house which faced onto a pawn shop. There were quite of few of us now, three guitarists, one drummer, Thep the saxophonist, a Filipino called Philip on trumpet, two female singers, and Tui who also sang, and who was the eldest son of the manager. We played there for a couple of months but were gradually paid less and less. However I always enjoyed Udorn. For one thing I got plenty of opportunity to practice my bowling. The two movie theatres, Chalermwattanarama and Vistarama, both had really good bowling facilities on their second floors, with plenty of lanes.

I was lucky enough to be able to visit the American camp because the Shang Gri-la bar owner, where we next played, was the 'wife' of the sergeant who ran the officer's club in the base. She put in a good word for us and we were invited to play at the base on Phupan Mountain. My father was visiting me at that time and was more than delighted to accompany us. Strippers were also organised for the show and we all bundled ourselves and our equipment into a large bus to make the treacherous journey on a dusty winding road that seemed mostly under repair. The three sides of the mountain were nearly vertical and I did not enjoy the drive. Neither did the strippers, and there was a lot of praying interjected with screams and hysterical giggling. However, my father absolutely loved it and kept trying to make me look out the window so that I could appreciate the heights we were climbing. When we reached the mountain top there was a helicopter parked outside the camp's entrance, and there was plenty of barbed wire. A pilot I knew told me that there were three security barriers; barbed wire, and beyond that an electric fence, and lastly a fence that was alarmed to the hilt. I saw lots of machine guns almost covered in their bunkers by gunny bags. Because of the height of the mountain it was quite misty, but you could not fail to appreciate the size of this military base.

We had also played at the military base in Udorn when we played at the non-commissioned officer's (NCO) bar. It was huge, with bomb shelters, bowling alleys and cinemas, and was completely staffed by Thai people, house-keepers, gardeners, cooks and waitresses. There was also a Laundromat staffed by Thai women. Oil was obviously something that they had in abundance; I remember my surprise at seeing three gardeners using three lawn mowers to do one small field. There was even a row of slot machines in the clubhouse. I felt really at home in my Elvis-style get up.

The Americans on the mountain were mostly technicians and they ran the place like no other camp I knew. For one thing they had a pet, a young brown bear, and they seemed to live on a ridiculous amount of eggs. Also the men didn't wear uniforms. This military base was not what it appeared and I learned much later about its tragic end. It was actually a secret Air Force radar facility sitting on one of the highest mountains around. There were links with bases in Laos, but as Laos was a neutral country, no foreign troops were meant to be based there. To avoid the detection of US soldiers crossing back and forth between the borders, it was decided that the site could only accommodate civilians or military personnel with civilian documentation. However the American Air Force didn't want to supply its men with false documents as it would cause majors problems if the men were captured, and they would have no protection under the Geneva Convention as prisoners of war.

Therefore the men had to be 'sheep dipped'. They left the Air Force and as civilians they were hired by a legitimate civilian company. Their employer sent them into Laos as ordinary employees. Afterwards they could rejoin the Air Force. The men were specially chosen for the mission.

It was believed that this location, high in the mountains, would protect the base from attack. The mountain was so steep that the Americans were confident their men would have plenty of time to be rescued by helicopter should their position be located by the Vietnamese. The secret radar was even wired up to explosives should the enemy attack. I don't remember seeing it myself but even if I did I would not have known what I was looking at.

It happened in March in 1968, just before midnight. 33 North Vietnamese managed to climb the mountain while enemy planes overhead were attempting to bomb the radar system. The Vietnamese had been practising climbing difficult rock peaks for months. When they reached the site, between the radar buildings and a Thai guard post, they hid until 3am. Then they made a move but were spotted by a guard who threw a grenade at them. This prompted the Vietnamese to open fire with their submachine guns. They killed over half the Americans they found there, men I had probably chatted to and certainly played in front of.

**

As usual the show on Phupan went down really well and we got plenty of cheers and applause. After the gig we all headed back to town for dinner. We had learned to behave ourselves when we were out late at night in the city. Plenty of high-spirited evenings ended in alcohol-fuelled battles so it was wise to keep to your own group and not attract any unpleasant attention. I wasn't happy. The Americans had paid quite a bit for us, but I only got a few hundred baht from the managers. I had also discovered that the Las Vegas bar had paid an advance of 2,000 baht before we even arrived in Udorn, none of which found its way into my pocket. That was the last straw and I quit the band.

I decided to head to Korat or Nakhon Ratchasima, north of Bangkok, with my girlfriend Tew. It was a busy enough town with plenty of shops and nightspots. I took a room at the Tokyo Hotel for 40 baht a night. An old friend from home and his girlfriend moved in with relatives of his who owned the Lucky Bar. I had thought that we might get to play in this bar but entertainment was provided by their compact and reliable jukebox. However, his girlfriend's uncle owned a bar and I got to play there. After maybe three weeks I returned to Bangkok. The uncle couldn't afford to pay us much and I had had to leave the hotel as I couldn't make the rent.

Back in Bangkok I was unemployed again and I accepted any little gig I could get, from weddings to birthday parties. I played briefly for a band called Johnny Guitar. We travelled to Nakhon Phanom to play at a movie-theatre near the Thai-Laos Border. I got tired of waiting for other people to throw me a bone and decided to form my own band, once again. There were five of us; Kay, who was a great guitarist, and the singers, husband and wife Klelk and Toi, Tui the drummer and myself on guitar. I suppose I hoped to recapture the good old days with Mitra but it wasn't meant to be. For our first gig in Ratchaburi, west of Bangkok, we got paid absolutely nothing, having been ripped off by the unscrupulous bar owner. I decided to try our luck at Ta Khli, and had got us a booking at the Blue Sky bar. This turned out to be a bar only frequented by African Americans. We didn't see one farang cross its threshold, which I found a bit strange.

I was also dealing with insecurities over my guitar playing—the band's and mine. As I say Kay was really good and Tui was a really talented drummer. They were all old friends of mine from Bangkok and it was galling to be made aware, by them, of the gap between their skill and mine. I no longer felt comfortable with them on stage. Furthermore, relations in the group were becoming a little strained. Tew, who was my girlfriend at the time, was now travelling with me to all our venues and she just didn't get on with Toi. They eventually had a full-blown argument one night in Ta Khli, which didn't help matters at all. Then there was the matter of our shaky finances. Toi had arranged for us to be supplied with most of our equipment in advance of making any money, and we weren't anyway near paying for it yet. And just when I felt that things really couldn't get any worse, my father arrived at the bar to tell me that the friend who lent me his cymbal now wanted it back. That was it, I threw in the towel. I am only human after all.

It turned out to be a wise move because shortly after my return to Bangkok I was asked to join The Crickets, a popular Thai tribute band to The Beatles. We played at the best of venues, like the Lido nightclub in Bangkok. This was a big nightclub, run by a Chinese guy, Sia-uan, who rented it from a police officer. It hosted a variety of shows, from magic to strippers, to dancing. There were lots of girls, mostly Thai or Japanese. I had a great time working there. A huge party was organised for New Year's Day and all the entertainers received gifts. I think I got a horse-shoe ash-tray and a wallet which I gave to my father. I even appeared with The Crickets on TV, when we performed 'Simple Simon Says' for the well-known *Seven Show*.

But of course, all good things come to an end. I was no longer a teenager, free of responsibility. The wild hey-day, if you could call it that, of the Vietnam War was coming to an end, and with it went my career as a musician. I needed to find a new path.

CHAPTER 3

My life had changed considerably by 1969. I had met Tew the previous year. She was 18 and I was 20. We lived near each other in Udorn. I shared a rented house on the Mhakkaeng Road while she lived next door, across from the pawn shop, with her cousins. I used to frequent a Kaogaeng stall on my way to work. This is a bit like fast food Thai-style—you choose two or three dishes and the owner spoons them on to a plate of rice.

I saw her there one day, sitting by herself and reading *Bangkok Magazine,* a popular rag magazine at the time. She was wearing a light summer blouse, khaki pants and her hair was held in place by a brightly coloured bandana. I watched her read for a while and thought about my approach. An idea popped into my head and I sidled up to her and asked could I borrow her magazine. Not very original I suppose, but it was the best I could come up with. However, when she smiled warmly at me in reply I knew I 'was in'. We developed a true friendship, with lots of conversation and exchanging of books and opinions. Our courtship consisted of dinners, movies and shopping. She was a typical northeast girl who was very attached to her family. And I liked that about her. She was, and still is, sincere and unpretentious. I always felt comfortable around her, plus she had a nice jaw-line—I don't know why, but I really dislike women with big jaw bones.

Tew was attractive without any of that sophistication and seductive beauty that can cause a lot of trouble for a man. I remember discreetly looking at her face and then studying my own in the mirror before reckoning that our children would probably be handsome enough. I didn't have to worry about her flirting with my friends behind my back; she was a practical girl who had fortunately decided to settle for me. I also felt ready to settle down after my years of travelling around. Plus, and I know this will sound very unromantic and selfish, but I really wanted someone who would look after my father, who was now in his 70s. She returned to Bangkok with me and got on like a house on fire with him.

We were a bit ahead of our time in that we lived together first. My father warned me not to mess her around, as she would find it difficult to meet someone else after living with me. She ran away from her cousins in Udorn to join me. We had kept our relationship secret from her family for as long as we could but of course that wasn't going to last forever. We only formally registered for marriage after the birth of our second son. Looking back now I just wish I had more money starting out. We probably rushed things unnecessarily. I don't remember us ever sitting down properly to discuss our future, and we had no savings between us, or a house, but I suppose it all worked out fine in the end.

My music career ended after I was summoned to do my military service and ended up in the Air Force. Given the choice, I would have preferred to continue playing guitar, but there wasn't really a choice. Two years was the legal requirement. I was glad that Tew was going to be at home minding my father. The aviation school, which was brand new, was in Nakhon Prathom, and again I did very well—I came first in the class. I lived on the base Monday to Friday and returned home to Bangkok every weekend. The dormitories were upstairs over the offices.

The training was very tough and I can't say that I enjoyed military life. It was all about toughening us up. On the first day we were told to leave our ego and status outside on the street because everyone was a just a soldier as far as school was concerned. The worst part for me was having to get up at 4.30 every morning, dress quickly, and then line up for inspection prior to running a few miles before breakfast. The training could mess with my head. At lunch we might all rush in hungrily to be fed but find that we had to line up in the canteen. We would be allowed in to sit down and our lunch would be dished out to us. Only we weren't allowed to eat it. Instead we would be taunted and asked if we were hungry? Did the food smell delicious? To which we had to reply with a resounding, 'No Sir!'

It was the same when we were out on one of those endless runs. Your lungs might be in a state of collapse or your leg could be broken in three places but woe betide anyone who answered in the affirmative when asked if they were tired. I couldn't believe the amount of running involved. Most of us needed new combat boots before the first year was up. Once again music saved me; I spent most of my free time playing my guitar.

***

That year saw many changes in my life. There was a death and a birth in my family. Sadly, my father died on Sunday 6 July, aged 77. I had arrived home on the Friday evening. As usual he was delighted to see me and had a lovely dinner ready. He seemed perfectly fit; he still rode his bicycle and enjoyed smoking his pipe after a meal. I asked him to help me make paper hats for a football match at the aviation school and he was delighted to help. On Saturday evening he was confused and distressed, saying he couldn't find 200 baht that he had stored somewhere in the house. I helped him look for it, or what was left of it after the termites had been feasting on the banknotes. I'm afraid that I got really annoyed and pointed out the mess and dirt of the house.

He didn't say anything, just hung his head in shame. Later on he listened to his favourite radio programme and danced to the songs he knew. He had been doing this for years. Around 9pm he said he had a stomach ache, and Tew also complained of not feeling well, so

I headed out to the chemist to get medicine. When I got back, my brother Oud had arrived in from work. After a while, everyone went to bed and I tidied up the house for an hour or so.

I awoke at 6am the following morning to a stricken Oud telling me that our father was dead. I wouldn't believe him. Tew and I rushed into his bedroom. For the first time ever he appeared painfully thin and frail to me, and deathly still. Oud left us to run and fetch the doctor. I broke down as I looked upon the lifeless body—the first dead body I had ever seen—and Tew clung to me as I wept. After a while Oud re-appeared with the doctor who confirmed he had died after his gallbladder burst. Oud said he heard him go to the bathroom several times during the night. Though this wasn't really out of the norm—for as long as I remember he always had to make several nocturnal visits to the bathroom.

When I think about it now it seems that news of his death spread almost immediately, and we were suddenly invaded by neighbours and friends. Oud was great, he just kept busy organising everything. He rang all our relatives, but they weren't very helpful. They immediately started telling us what to do for the funeral—silly stuff like be sure to get a pretty coffin, book a band, or show a movie—but didn't us offer any money towards it. I think I was still too much in shock to be of any help; all I could focus on was that I needed to ask the aviation school for some time off. I walked out of the house amid family trying to locate someone to embalm my father's body, which was still warm to the touch.

I remember crying all the way to the school over the worry of how we were going to pay for the funeral. I had no savings and Oud had little more than me. I turned up at the Commander's house and told him that I needed time off because my father had just died. He asked to see the death certificate, which of course I never thought to bring with me. Fortunately he could see that I was genuinely stricken with grief.

We kept his body at home, that old rundown house that he loved. He had always said he wanted to die at home, so I was going to keep him here as long as I could. Besides, he was scared of hospitals and refused to go near one after his first wife had died during a minor operation—I don't think he ever got over that. For months after, I blamed myself for not making him go to hospital when he complained he wasn't well. I know he would have argued that we couldn't afford it but maybe if I had got him to the hospital they might have treated him, because it was an emergency, and let me pay afterwards, I would have got the money together eventually.

My father was certainly a popular and well-respected man. I was persuaded to move his body to the Wat, the Buddhist temple, because the house couldn't hold the crowds that came to pay their respects. Oud and I hosted the funeral. We didn't have much money and were grateful to the large number of people who gave us thousands of baht towards the expense. My father had already given me a list of phone numbers of his former students that I was to call if ever I was stuck. His faith in his students was justified. I rang Manoon Trirat to tell him the news. He turned up for the funeral with many other former students, that he had personally contacted, and was a huge help to us. They all gave us money and Manoon offered us books about the moon and space travel to be given out as a keepsake of the funeral. Usually people would give out books on Buddhism but Neil Armstrong was about to go to the moon and everyone I knew was really excited about it. Pat Boonratpan, the Governor of Ubolratchathani, flew in specially and took charge of the proceedings one night. You see, Thai funerals run for several days. Phra Manoowes, a senior member of the Privy Council, also came to pay his respects and my mother turned up and made Malai, a traditional Thai flower arrangement.

As one life departed, so another came into my world. My son, Prawes, was born at 5.17am on Thursday, 30 October. The new arrival helped to fill the void caused by my father's death, though I couldn't help wishing that he had lived to see his grandson. I only got to see him, myself, late on Friday evening when I returned from the Air Force. Tew was still very tired but very proud of this tiny little being. It took a lot of encouragement on her part to get me to hold him; I was terrified that I might break him. I'm sure most men think that when they are faced with their first child, plus I don't think that I had ever held a newborn baby before. Anyway I was completely smitten; he was the most beautiful thing I had ever seen—at least until his siblings arrived. I was a lot more confident with the other two children, once they came along.

**

I started to study Para medicine in the medical department of the Air Force and did well in the exams. I worked at Jantarubeksa Hospital in the Kampaengsaen district of Nakhon Prathom. There weren't a lot of doctors or nurses there so I had to work hard. It was a little overwhelming if there was something big like a train crash. However, it was a good training experience from doing first aid to assisting with operations.

I learned a lot of things during my time there. For the first time I observed a clear division between men based on their background and military status. It struck me that education was an important tool—life in the army wasn't so rewarding if you hadn't got a decent education. I decided not to pursue a career in the Forces and was impatient for my two-year stint to end. I was offered the chance to further my medical studies but I just longed to return to the stage and the big money.

I graduated on 30 April 1971. Shortly after the ceremony I called up my old band mates and we headed out to the Playboy bar in Ubol. Unfortunately it was all different now. The Americans had gone and business was bad. The owner paid us for our first two nights but on our third he paid us less than what he promised, and on the fourth and fifth night he had no money to give us at all. A lot of the bars and restaurants were closed due to lack of business. We tried our luck in Korat but the bar owner there couldn't afford to pay us, and neither could the owner in Ta Khli. I decided to cut my losses and return home to Bangkok.

My older brother was working in a bar in Patpong and I would often drop in on him. I was worried about making a living and supporting my young family. A friend of ours, Na, opened a bar in her house at Lang Suan behind Erawan Hotel. One night my brother introduced me to her boyfriend George, an American, who introduced me to his buddy Bob Clarson. Bob was head of the oil survey team that worked for Thailand and Singapore. I couldn't believe my luck when he told me that he might have a job for me.

I ended up on an island off Pattanee, a province in the south of Thailand, working for a bad-tempered American. Up to now my experiences with farangs had all been positive but this was about to change. I was employed as an interpreter for the natural gas survey team, which meant giving Tew as much money as I could spare before stocking up on three months worth of canned food. My boss and I had to set up a radio station in order to communicate with the ships out drilling for gas and also with the headquarters in Singapore. There was lots of equipment that I had never used before so naturally I was a bit hesitant. He would just shout at me, impatient at my ignorance instead of showing me what he wanted me to do. Most of the farangs there yelled at their Asian counterparts and treated them as if they were stupid. There was a pattern to their behaviour; they would insult you first and then they would pat you on the head or the back and all would be fine again, until the next time.

I couldn't believe the amount of money that was spent on ridiculous things. Once a guy was flown in from Singapore just to fix a transistor radio. They spent 200 baht in sending me back to Pattanee to buy an unnecessary, in my opinion, spare part. I was quite suspicious about their expenses and their desire to spend as much money as possible but I was in no position to question it.

Soon I was very fed up—it was boring and I missed my family in Bangkok. It was hard to sleep at night thanks to the mosquitoes and I was forced to take long walks when my boss wanted to be alone with his Thai girlfriend. Every day was the same—make coffee for the boss, eat, swim in the sea and inevitably be yelled at for something or other. I had no choice but to stick it out, I needed the money. Finally in June I was told that the mission was completed and that we could start packing up. I was delighted to be going home. I met up with Bob back in Bangkok. He bought me a beer in

Na's bar at Langsuan House, where I was living, and paid me 1400 baht.

I found myself unemployed once again.

Then, on 21 July 1971, a couple of weeks later, my older cousin Too rang me up to tell me that the Department of Corrections in the Ministry of Interior was looking for prison guards. He suggested that I meet him the following day and he would help me fill out the application form. And I thought to myself, why not ..?

CHAPTER 4

In 1902, King Rama V bought a large piece of land in Nonthaburi to build a prison for long-term prisoners. Construction only started in 1927, after his death, and under the rule of King Rama VI, and was completed in 1931. Today Bang Kwang Central Prison holds three types of prisoners: prisoners whose appeals are pending in the Appeal Court and the Supreme Court; prisoners who are serving a sentence of 25 years or more, and the 'death sentence' prisoners. The prison was only ever intended to hold 4,000 prisoners, but today it holds more than twice that.

It is strange. My father was always so supportive of me and followed me around Thailand whenever he could to watch me play with the various bands, but I am glad he didn't live to see me enter this new phase of my life. He wouldn't have liked to see me in a prison guard's uniform, as he looked down on the guards and believed them to be a rough, vulgar lot.

I had told my brother Oud about the job vacancies and persuaded him that he should at least apply too. He agreed to but wasn't very enthusiastic. The following morning we met our cousin Too at Sanam Luang and went to the Ministry of Interior to pick up the application forms. We needed a letter from our doctor so we headed over to Tah Phrajan, but his office was closed. I gritted my teeth in frustration while Oud merely shrugged his shoulders. Then Too brought us over to Klong Prem Central Prison to ask a friend of his, Rabiab Supokiawanich, who was a senior guard, to sign both our forms as guarantor. That evening my brother and I went to a doctor in Pratunam for our medical. After a thorough examination he gave us a clean bill of health.

I posted off our forms the next day, after attaching passport photos and doctor's certificate. Too was fairly confidant that we would be called to attend the examination. I met up with him a few times so that he could take me through the different questions asked and give me pointers. Sure enough, on 16 August, the Minister of Interior released the names of the applicants who were to do the exam and issued them with their examination numbers. I was number 72 and Oud was 58. We were to attend the Arts building at Thammasart University on 11 September, where we had to undergo a two-day examination as well as an intensive interview. The exam consisted of four papers spread over the two days. The first one concerned general knowledge followed by the afternoon paper on the rights and duties of the individual in society. The third paper concerned law, corrective law in particular. The last paper involved the rules and regulations of a being a prison guard.

I went home determined to pass. Too had given me his books and I buried myself in them. I was really meticulous in my study; I took pages and pages of notes, and set myself questions that I had to answer in a certain amount of time. Then I used a tape-recorder to tape myself reading aloud possible questions with the right answers so that I could listen and hopefully absorb the answers into my subconscious as I went about my day. I read and re-read those books until I could practically say them in my sleep. I did my best to help Oud. He found it quite tough to do any study since his typical working day in the bar didn't finish until three, sometimes four, in the morning.

In no time at all, or so it seemed, the morning of 11 September dawned. Poor Oud had to cram for hours the night before, after telling his boss that he was too sick to work. That was a drama in itself when George, his boss, wanted to know exactly what was wrong with him. Two months earlier Oud's eyes took on a yellow hue and his boss made him go to doctor. It turned out he was in the early phase of cirrhosis of the liver and had to go on a course of medicine immediately. George's girlfriend's niece was studying nursing and he asked her for information on the condition. Obviously thrilled to be asked her professional opinion, while still a student, she wrote him a letter furnishing him with more detail than was perhaps required. As a result, when George was told that Oud was sick again, and after he was reassured that it wasn't life threatening, he forbade anyone to visit him while he was ill.

We were just two of a total of 707 people who were taking the exam. It was tough enough. I felt I might have scrapped a pass, but Oud wasn't as positive. Interviews for those numbered between one and one hundred were held on the following Monday, 13 September. Oud went in first and came out sweating. One of the questions had thrown him: 'Where was the Emerald Buddha'?

He just couldn't think of the answer which unnerved him for the rest of the interview. Of course, everybody knew the Emerald Buddha was a famously valuable Buddha made of nephrite jade. Its true value was discovered in the 15th century after it fell and its gold-leaf coating cracked open to reveal the green rock. It moved around a lot but was now kept in the Buddhist temple called Wat Phragaew in Bangkok. Oud just couldn't remember this, and this made me even more nervous than I already was. However, it didn't turn out to be as bad as I expected. They mostly asked me personal questions. Too had warned me that they would be testing me for my reactions or solutions to different scenarios.

The weeks dragged by and finally, on 10 November, we got our results. Out of the 707 applicants, Oud came 311th and I came 122nd. Too was delighted when he heard, and I invited him over to my house for dinner that night to celebrate and thank him for all his help. We reckoned that I would probably get a position in the second round of the hiring process. I was very proud of myself. After the whole experience working with my American boss, a button had been pressed inside of me. I knew that I never wanted to work for farangs again; I had found the whole experience demeaning and unpleasant. I didn't ever want to be in a job that left me open to insults and put-downs. Being a prison guard wasn't a fancy job, nor was the pay a huge amount, but I saw it as a respectable government job, and one that I gotten through my own capabilities. I felt that it would suit me and my personality. My father had taught me to treat people as I would like to be treated in turn, so I could achieve things within the role of prison guard, and improve the position.

Finally on 27 December 1971 the journey was over. I was to report to the Ministry of Interior on 10 January 1972, when I would begin my new job. That morning I found myself standing among a crowd of successful applicants in a cramped room, on the first floor of the Ministry. We were waiting to be told where we were going to work. I was hoping to be sent to Klong Prem and my heart sank a bit when I heard my name called out with nine others who were assigned to Bang Kwang prison. My new colleagues, six men and three women, and I immediately headed back out into the heat of morning sun to take the bus to Nonthaburi Watchtower, which is near the prison. We talked a little amongst ourselves and I suppose we were all a bit nervous. Some of the louder ones talked about beating up any inmates who gave them a hard time but I don't think they meant it. They were just trying to reassure themselves.

I had never really taken much notice of the prison when I was growing up. It was a landmark like any other, and I gave it as much attention as I gave the opium houses, or maybe less so. Now that I was about to enter it for the very first time I noted everything in the minutest detail. The walls were huge and seemed to go on forever—in fact they are 2,406 metres long and six metres high.

We made our way to the general office where we were welcomed by the Slab Visutthimuk, the superintendent. He was quite pleasant and asked us a few questions about our education, work experience and skills. There were vacancies in all the different sectors within the prison, such as administration, prisoner's welfare, teaching and religious instruction, and prison warden. After spending some time with us he decided who was best suited for what. Basically the girls ended up in the pen-pushing departments while the guys and I headed to the custody section to meet another boss, Manoo Nargvichian. My first responsibilities were to search the prisoners for weapons and drugs when they went in and out of the different buildings, and make sure they were wearing their uniforms correctly, and

I had to train the 'assistants', the fierce inmates chosen to help the prison officers in keeping a firm control of the jail. Their official name was 'trustee'.

***

It is the smell of pig shit that hits you first. Livestock were kept to the left of the prison's entrance, in what was known as the vocational training area. However, that smell was no where as bad as the smell inside the prison. I thought I was going to be sick that first day. I do remember being seriously worried that I wouldn't be able to stick it out. It's hard to say which was worse—the stench of urine, shit, stale sweat, or rotting foodstuff.

I wasn't allowed to patrol the wings of the prison until I had spent a month getting to know the place. Patrolling could be a risky business; a guard had been killed after finding a prisoner attempting to escape. For the first few weeks I only patrolled in the company of a senior officer. We were told never to turn our backs on a prisoner because it would give him the chance to hit you, and we were also told never to stop a fight in case we got hurt. There was an evening and night shift—basically the jail had to be patrolled from 4.30 in the morning to 6am the following morning. This would be divided into three sections: 4.30am – 12pm, 12pm – 3am and 3am to 6am. We would take turns covering the different stages. It was quite strict when I started. You had to walk quietly and not let your keys jangle together. Any guard who fell asleep on his shift would be reported. I think it is different today, a bit more laid-back. The guards today can watch TV, which was unheard of when I first started patrolling.

I was very apprehensive about meeting the prisoners themselves. I had always been careful to stay away from trouble and now I was going to be dealing with hardened criminals. Some of them were definitely rough looking but in fact they were quite well behaved. They knew the rules and most just wanted to keep their heads down and get on with it. It was a big enough job trying to get on with other prisoners without wilfully pissing off the guards. There were the normal power struggles as in any society. Someone who committed a murder thought he was toughest until the next one bragged that he had killed 12, and so on. As I got used to the job and the prisoners I reasoned that it didn't matter how notoriously bad they had been on the outside, now they all had to wear shorts and address me as sir.

Their lives revolved around routine. The day began at 6am with breakfast. At 8.30am prisoners, who wished to, attended the various vocational training workshops or classes. Lunch was at mid-day, followed by more classes at 1pm until 3.30pm. Then there was an hour of recreation for personal activities. Some enjoyed sports or just worked out to keep fit. Dinner was at 4.30pm and at 5.30pm the prisoners were locked back into their cells for the evening. The prisoners were supposed to sleep from 9pm but they usually stayed up until midnight chatting. They had an easier time than prisoners did years ago. In the early days there were no humanitarian organisations keeping an eye on conditions. Nowadays, officers cannot hit inmates and there has also been quite a furore over the wearing of leg irons. The chains are smaller and lighter today and are only used on death row prisoners or on prisoners likely to try and escape. It is the Ministry of Interior who decides whether a prisoner should be chained up or not. Female convicts are not required to wear chains. The shackles were formerly used as an extra punishment for being in prison, now they are more about preventing escape.

I wasn't interested in befriending the prisoners. One of them did ask me where I was from and was delighted to hear me say Nonthaburi, as that was where he was from. I was very strict in those early days and had no real interest in the men yet. Over time I would wonder what brought them to the jail. I attended seminars on criminality and read up on the cases of the prisoners to understand them better. Fortunately I didn't have to patrol as much as the others. I spent a lot of time in my office liaising with the 'helpers' which I felt made me look authoritative and gave me a bit of leverage with the rest of the prisoners.

Managing the 'assistants' was a good job and I was appreciative of it. I was given it on account of my army training and experience. These inmates were like the highest-ranking prisoners—they didn't live with the rest of the prisoners, instead they had their own little dormitories which were located in front of Wings 5 and 6. They were my own army of 30 men who had to do my bidding. Of course it wasn't going to be easy. I had to make my mark first, though only one guy gave me some attitude because I was a rookie. Some papers had fallen all over the floor and I asked him to pick them up. He refused and said it wasn't his job. I said nothing and just smiled at him, and waited.

On Saturday I summoned all the assistants to my office. I told them that I wanted them to check around the Bang Kwang wall just to make sure all was normal. Not everyone heeded my call. A few of the helpers decided to visit their friends in other wings, this being a Saturday. I was gratified to see that my awkward friend was one of these. I reported all the absentees to my superior with the suggestion that they lose their privileged position. The men who had turned up went running for their friends to warn them. I received quite a few desperate apologies over the next hour but I didn't care. I wanted to make an impression that I wasn't to be messed with. The absentees lost out and were sent back to live in the wings; after that nobody tried to test me again.

***

I certainly would not have wanted to live there. Prison life is extremely stressful. You wear the same clothes every day. You share a cell at night-time, and during the day a small room, with far too many other men. Imagine trying to sleep at night with all the snoring, groaning and coughing. They even shower together in groups, in open areas. In the day-time you have to use the toilet in front of your room-mates; there is no toilet door, only a wall that is waist high—to prevent suicides. Although, a few years ago if you needed to take a dump when you were in the cell, you had to sit on a wooden bucket and then clean yourself using a bottle of water kept for that purpose. Arguments would start when sleeping inmates were inevitably hit with bits of shit because they were so near the bucket, through lack of floor space. Now we have toilets in the cells along with small bowls of water.

If you didn't have any money to supplement basic rations you were in trouble. A prisoner is fed three meals a day for only 27 baht, so it is impossible to serve up decent meals for that amount. Prisoners could lose a serious amount of weight and succumb to every bug and virus going. Vicious fights would break out over the simplest of things, like changing the TV channel. Many prisoners would try to form a group of sorts so that they would be afforded some protection from the bullies. Others would try to strike up an allegiance with a guard. It was all about perception; you had a better chance of surviving if you made yourself look powerful.

It's the constant threat of warfare that I could not have coped with. Like any where else there are good and bad inmates. The good ones, who had broken the law unintentionally or just the one unlucky time, usually took advantage of the vocational training programmes that the jail offered—they could even study for a university degree. They looked for jobs within Bang Kwang and put aside their small earnings in a no-interest savings account. They could then afford to buy food or toiletries at the prison shop, or else they could keep their money for when they had completed their sentence. The bad guys were the ones who were living criminal lives on the outside and only know how to make money from illegal activities. They tried to continue their careers on the inside by organizing gambling rackets. As I said, fights broke out frequently and could be very bloody. If an inmate stole another's shower gel there could be a stabbing. If someone started to play cards and ended up owing money he could not pay back there could be a stabbing.

The prison housed a variety of people, among them 'ladyboys'. These 'ladyboys' almost always caused bloody feuds. If an inmate thinks his 'girlfriend' (the Thai term of endearment is *nong*) is being flirted with by another all hell can break loose. The prison guards were on red alert when a new 'ladyboy' arrived because it usually meant a battle for the right to gain her hand 'in matrimony'. They tended to treat their 'girlfriends' very well, and shared any food or parcels that they received. In fact the prison prefers not to accept them anymore because it is much too risky for the ladyboy. Their being raped is almost inevitable. They would need 24-hour protection which we would not be able to stretch to. They were usually only guilty of relatively small-time offences like possessing a minor amount of soft drugs or pick-pocketing. The majority of them were prostitutes, though they stopped short of sex. The story was always the same. The client was lured to a room and offered a drink containing sleeping pills. When they would wake a few hours later they would probably be missing their wallets, watch and shoes, if they were expensive. Ladyboys weren't allowed to wear their hair long in Bang Kwang and when they took a bath they usually wore a *grajhom-ok*, a garment which covered their breasts if they had any. In Thailand, women wear a skirt high on their body to cover their breasts when bathing in a river, and the ladyboys did the same in Bang Kwang, out of shyness at bathing in front of men.

They could be good fun and liven up the atmosphere. I remember once when some 'ladyboys' put on a show in the auditorium. They got hold of wigs and elaborate dresses and performed the can-can amongst other things. They got a great reception that night and were as excited as chattering four-year-olds who had just received their birthday presents all at once.

But they can also cause trouble in other ways. An angry prisoner's wife once complained to a prison guard that her husband was having an affair with a '*katoey*' (offensive term for 'ladyboys'). She was enraged and told the guard that her husband didn't love her anymore, and if that wasn't bad enough she learnt that all the presents she had brought to him in prison were being given, in turn, to her rival. It was as well that the 'ladyboy' was behind bars as the wife was well built and fearsome looking.

Prison taught me that loneliness will drive a man to do strange things. I remember when one of the inmates decided to try his luck and wrote to a magazine's dating column. There was great excitement among his cell mates when he received a reply from a woman. He told her that he had been jailed because he accidentally killed the guy who raped his sister—an honourable crime indeed and complete fiction. Anyway the woman believed him and had great sympathy for his dilemma which led to him being in Bang Kwang. She was very eager and after a few letters, which were read aloud to his friends, went back and forth she suggested coming to visit him in prison. Even the prison guards got caught up wondering what she looked like. The date was set and the guy fixed himself up as much as he could, considering the circumstances. Well she exceeded everyone's expectations, so much that the prisoner panicked. He obviously had no faith in his own appearance and hastily hired a good-looking prisoner to meet with her in his place. It also transpired that he had hired another prisoner to write all his letters for him so the poor girl had not actually dealt with him in any way. He was teased for ages afterwards and couldn't answer the obvious question; why on earth had he bothered writing to the magazine in the first place?

***

I should probably describe the prison: It's like a big college campus. As I said, the livestock and vocational training facilities are to the left of the prison's entrance. They take up a lot of space but then they need to be big as they serve over 8,000 prisoners. On the right is the car park which faces on to the football field. To the extreme right of the football field is the large auditorium, complete with a stage. Behind this is the solitary confinement area which is not really used so much now. If you walk in a straight line from the prison entrance you would pass the visiting rooms on your right and left. You would walk past the 7-storey security tower's door and then find yourself looking at the wings. There would be a sort of junction where the security tower stands, and just beside that the Custody Section building where I used to have my office. There is another watch tower at the outer wall behind Wing 4.

There are six wings in total; wings 4, 5 and 6 to your right-hand side and then wings 1, 2 and 3 to your left. Also to your right, just in front of wings 4, 5 and 6 are the two small dormitories for the assistants to the prison guards. Each wing holds between 800 and 1000 prisoners. Wing 1 holds the prisoners who have received the death penalty. Behind wings 1, 2 and 3 is the prison clinic where sick prisoners are kept. If you continue on past the wings you reach a large storage facility which is also used to die clothes. Uniforms, soap, crockery and paint thinners are kept here. Then, if you turn left here you find yourself looking at the kitchen, which is staffed by prisoners from Wing 4.

Just past the kitchen is the wooden diamond-shaped gazebo where prisoners are brought before their execution. A table is usually set up with flowers and incense to calm the condemned. The execution room is beyond the gazebo, and looks more like a white wooden shed with a large front porch. There is a good bit of green grass around it and under other circumstances it might be described as pretty. The sign over the porch roughly translates into English as 'the place to end all sorrow'. The morgue is just a tiny room of to the right that was mostly empty. There is a door on the left hand side of the building which is called 'ghost's door' since it is used to bring bodies out into the temple for cremation. There used to be a statue of Yommaban at the entrance to the execution room, and prisoners would have to pass it on their way in. Thais believed that this spirit punished the wicked in the afterlife. Personally I found the statue and the sign to be in extremely poor taste.

Just beyond then is the Wat Bangpraktai, what you might call a temple—a big building with a red roof which could be clearly seen as you approached the execution room. I suppose it may have proved a comforting sight to a prisoner who was making his last journey. The temple houses the abbot or chaplain and is quite separate from the day-to-day running of the jail. When an execution is to take place a guard would be sent around to invite the abbot to perform the last rites.

The 'death row' Wing has received many visits from journalists and camera crews. Here a journalist speaks to the camera live from the wing with a typical description;

'Right now, I'm standing in the area that houses the prisoners on death row. It's safe to say that this is the centre of Bang Kwang Prison. There are 280 convicts here, divided among 24 cells. The number of convicts in each cell varies from seven to 15. I am now waling into a room where 14 convicts are kept. The room is about three by seven metres. There is a small toilet here behind a wall that is only waist-high, there is no door. The only other thing in the room is a rubbish bin. The bars of the cell are made of thick metal and they are about four inches apart. The floor is bare cement. Light is provided by fluorescent tubes on the ceiling between the cells, but it is still quite dim.'

***

In Bang Kwang, every morning hundreds of prisoners come out of the cells and they all have to be searched for drugs, money or weapons. We were helped in this task by our 'assistants'. We needed them because there just weren't enough guards to do all that was required.

Over the years I found a surprising amount of stuff on the prisoners: cash, opium, marijuana, and harder drugs like heroin. Drugs are a huge problem in the prison. Understandably there a lot of inmates suffering from terrible depression that neither religion nor playing football can help them fight. They turn to drugs for some sort of escape. Then there are the foreign prisoners who complain to their embassies that they can't sleep. The embassy supplies them with a large batch of sleeping pills—valium and lithium seem to be the drugs of choice— which may indeed be used by the inmate to help him sleep, but more often than not they are sold on to the other prisoners for a profit.

It's not a pleasant thing to have to do everyday— give hundreds of men a body search. The inmates are graded according to their behaviour. There is a choice of six grades; very bad, bad, middling, good, very good and excellent. The average inmate usually has a middling score. Anyone who breaks house rules can be punished in a number of ways. He might lose the right to receive visitors or he could be downgraded. Years ago a high grade made you eligible for amnesty if there was a Royal Pardon and your sentence could be cut in half. These pardons used to happen every second year but then the public began to complain that criminals weren't being jailed for long enough. Nowadays the pardons happen infrequently and sentences can only be reduced by one sixth—unless you are in jail for drug-related offences, in which case you will never be granted amnesty.

This downgrading usually took place in a court room. I appeared in court as a witness many times. The inmate would be represented by his lawyer and he would grill me as to how the prisoner obtained drugs in his cell. This question was always tricky for me but I would begin by pointing out that the prisoner wasn't completely isolated from the outside world. He could receive drugs in parcels from friends and relatives. We had already found drugs in strange places like toothpaste and shampoo bottles. Invariably I would find myself admitting that an alternative to parcels from outside was the prison guards themselves. There are corrupt people in all walks of life, it is simply a reality. Some guards could be bribed to collect drugs from suppliers on their days off. It always came down to the same thing—money.

Both inmates and guards were forbidden to carry cash in the prison. Officers had to empty their pockets before they went on duty. As for the prisoners, money would just cause extra headaches. The biggest problem was that a prisoner with ready cash would be tempted to bribe a guard to bring him in his drugs or even to escape. Then there were the other prisoners. If you had money you can be sure that someone else would try to take it from you. Therefore you would be endangering yourself as well as in-house law and order.

The guards could also be tricked into couriering drugs to the inmates. A prisoner would sometimes urge his 'favourite' guard to go to a particular bar or restaurant with assurances that he would be well looked after, because the owner was a friend of his. The prisoner might even write up a letter of introduction for the guard as further encouragement. The guard is persuaded and heads off, maybe on a Friday after work, to the venue in question and finds himself being utterly spoiled without having to put a hand in his pocket. Then after the guard has eaten and drank his fill for free he would be presented with a carton of cigarettes to bring back to their poor friend in prison. And maybe just one packet in that carton would be crammed with drugs, but how could the guard insult his generous host by refusing this simple errand?

Then there's the case of unfortunate Prayuth Sanun who was a prison guard that I liked and is now sentenced to the death penalty. His troubles began after he took a weekend job as a bouncer for extra money. He was hired by a popular restaurant. Bouncing usually entails being paid cash in hand, with instant respect from the men and attraction from the women. The most trying problem is probably persuading drunken teenagers that they have had enough. A bouncer can earn up to 400 baht a night, cash in hand. Prayuth enjoyed his new job and started to make all kinds of friends, including dangerous ones like mobsters, loan sharks and drug dealers. He found that his new associates were handy when things got out of control. You try barring someone from entering the venue, they are drunk or mad and get aggressive, you hit them and they leave, filling the air with threats and promises. True to their word they return with a gang of friends, all wanting to damage you. Now, that is the worst thing that can happen and you need friends near you in those circumstances. Then favours are done and repaid back and forth, and before you know it you are helping your new friends collecting monies owed, for which you need to start carrying a gun because now you have entered a vicious circle.

Prayuth says he was never asked out straight to start selling drugs, and neither does he remember exactly when he started to do it—one thing simply led to another. He soon came to the attention of the police who filmed his every movement. Eventually he was caught with 700,000 amphetamine tables, a M16 gun and lots of cash. Because he was a prison guard he received an even worse sentence. He has been on death row for six or seven years now. I could hardly look at him after he received his sentence. He was absolutely distraught. Prayuth was a good guy. You could rely on him if you had a problem. When he had money he would spend it on his friends.

But there are also corrupt guards. I would never deny that. A prison guards contacts a prisoner's relatives, which we are not allowed to do. He informs the family that their son, husband, brother, father, needs money and he will personally see that he gets it. And the prisoner does receive the money, albeit after the guard deducts his 'fee'. The family might even be encouraged to reward the guard for looking after their relative, with booze or perhaps a pretty young daughter or niece.

Of course I think a lot of the problem could have been dealt with by improving the wages of the prison guard. Back then I was getting 580 baht a month, which wasn't much with a growing family, especially since I wanted my kids to go to the better schools. To make ends meet I played gigs at the weekend and I suppose this was also a good escape for me. Music kept me sane in later years when the pressures of the job could have driven me to alcohol or worse. I even played for the prisoners and taught some of them to play guitar.

Whether you're carting in drugs to the prisoners or not you have to be aware of the part you play, as a prison officer, in contributing to their role-playing within the prison. I can simplify it down to two categories of inmates: the big egos and the small egos. Now the small-time crooks or first-time offenders do not give any trouble at all. They are usually too concerned with their own misery, and also many of them have been abandoned to their fates by friends and family. Others just think about getting through their sentence and then getting back to their lives outside. It is the big noises that you have to watch. We have had all sorts in the prison, from ex-generals to doctors. They lived important lives on the outside and they see no reason why they should be treated as any less important behind bars.

So they come in full of attitude. They look down on the prison guards, and will not actually engage with the guards who are younger than them. Instead they will demand to talk to the Superintendent. They talk loud and bold about who they know on the outside. Once, a guard wanted his child to get into a particularly up-market school. He approached one of these guys for help. The inmate wrote a letter and told the guard to give it to his local politician. He did and his kid was immediately accepted by the school. I don't think I would have done that. If you ask them for help you are pandering to them, and acknowledging their superiority to you. If they are so big and important, what are they doing in Bang Kwang? Also nobody does something for nothing. You can be sure that if those guys do you a favour they will want something in return, which could involve you risking your life by bringing in drugs.

The guard thinks he is having a friendly chat with the inmate who has just asked him what car he drives. When the guard admits to owing a very ordinary vehicle the inmate lights up and tells the guard that he drives a BMW and better yet he can help him become the proud owner of one because he knows a car-dealer. If you take his advice and seek out this dealer you will probably find that cars are not the only products he supplies.

A further headache for the prison guard is caused by the relatives. A father with money and power will have an important friend ring the Superintendent and tell him that he wants his son looked after inside. His wish is passed on to us and we have to treat the little fool with kid gloves. This gives him a big head and an ego boost in front of the other prisoners, and suddenly he is causing problems for the young and inexperienced guards because he knows that Daddy is just a phone-call away.

CHAPTER 5

20 December 1971.

Bangjak Subdistrict, Phrapradaeng District, Samutprakarn Province: The police station in Phrapradaeng receives a phone call from a farmer who has found a body on his coconut farm. Officers rush to the scene where the battered and torn body of ten-year-old Varee Songsuk lies in the mud. The autopsy report is difficult to read; her little body is covered in wounds and bruises. The hymen is torn and there is semen in the vagina, which is also bloodied and torn. There is extensive bruising to her neck and chin. Clay has been shoved down her throat as far as the larynx. The report concludes that she was strangled and then suffocated to death.

The following day the police arrest four young men aged between 14 and 21: Sane Oongaew, Somchai Sansuk, Cherdchai Praditsuwan and Narat Oongaew (Sane's younger brother). The three youngest immediately confess to the crime, and place Sane— who denies all charges—at the scene. They describe the previous night in detail.

On the night of 19 December 1971 Varee was crossing the street near where she lived, heading for Thaigrienggao Alley in Bangjak. Seven males in total grabbed the child who started to scream. They picked her up by her arms and legs, covered her mouth to stop her cries and carried her across Suksawat Road to a construction site where Sane was waiting to join them. They then continued with the struggling child on to the farm. When they reached a secluded spot two of the males, Cherdchai and Poom, pinned her arms and legs to the ground while Sane, Narat and another guy Eed took turns raping her. They were also trying to strangle Varee as they raped her. After the raping the eight males beat up the little girl, and stuffed up her mouth with dirt before running away.

The police discovered that 21-year-old Sane's father was the chief authority in the village of Bangjak. They were suddenly approached by villagers who had been too scared to report the many rapes committed by Sane against their women. Sane, who had become a monk, never ever admitted to committing even one rape and showed absolutely no sign of guilt or remorse.

Somchai, Cherdhai and Narat, aged 16, 15 and 14 respectively, were juveniles. It was also taken into consideration that they had co-operated fully with the police in their investigations. Cherdhai, in particular, who did not partake in the actual raping, had methodically taken the police through the sequence of horrific events. As a consequence, they received different prison sentences: Somchai Sansuk was sentenced to life imprisonment, Cherdchai Praditsuwan was sentenced to 15 years and Narat Oonkaew was sentenced to 25 years. Their prison terms were effective immediately. Sane Oonkaew, however, was sentenced to death by General Thanom Kittikajorn, head of the Revolution Committee. Once the execution order had been issued, the Director of National Security, Prapas Jarusatian, instructed the Ministry of Interior to carry it out immediately. The location of the execution was Bang Kwang Central Prison in Nonthaburi and the date was 9 February 1972.

***

I was excited. I had been working in Bang Kwang for less than 20 days and already I was going to witness an execution. The prison had an execution time-table which impacted on the normal routine. The execution team of ten to 12 officers was only announced the morning of an execution. The various roles included executioner, escort, gun adjuster and administrative— those two were to take the fingerprints, photograph the prisoner and assemble the records. Letters had to be written to certain officials, asking them to come and witness the execution. These guests could be an inspector from the DOC (Department of Corrections), the Governor of Nonthaburi, the chief of police and Attorney General in Nonthaburi, lawyers, and representatives from the Criminal Records section of the police departments.

Keeping detailed records and properly filing them away is imperative to the process. When a prisoner is sentenced to death we take their fingerprints and photos, which are sent to the Criminal Records section for verification. Their records are also checked for previous offences. Then all the information is sent to the DOC. 60 days after sentencing the condemned can submit an application for a more lenient penalty. The case will be discussed by a committee and if it fails the execution process resumes. The Ministry of Interior briefs the DOC which in turn contacts Bang Kwang, who usually receives the execution order at approximately 9am that morning. The letters go out to the witnesses and the Chaplain or abbot is told that his services will be required. He will perform the last rites.

Lunch is usually served an hour early, which means that all the prisoners know when there is to be an execution. They are then locked into their cells before the officials arrive. At 4pm the escorts will go to collect the prisoner, whose fingerprints and photos are taken again. Then the execution order is read to them and they have to sign it. After that they are offered paper and pen to write out their last letter or will for their families, followed by their last meal and then the last rites. By 5 or 6pm everything should be in place for the execution itself. During the reign of the Revolution Committee summary executions were announced on TV and radio after the evening news. On 8 February at 8pm it was broadcast to the nation that Sane Oonkaew was to be executed the following day, for the rape and murder of a young girl.

The next day the prison was surrounded by journalists and camera crews, all desperate for a shot of the condemned man. Some had even climbed on to the roof of the Buddhist temple, the temple where relatives usually cremated the body 24 hours after execution. The atmosphere in the prison was frantic, at least among the wardens. High ranking officers from the Department of Corrections, and other organizations, were coming to see the execution and the prison officers were running around making sure that everything was perfect.

The quietest part of the prison was the six wings; the inmates were silent and watchful. Officers were on high alert and took extra precautions in the face of possible riots and protests. There was also the fear that with all the fuss some gangsters on the outside might take the opportunity to break in and release their friends—especially those on death row.

At 4.30am I stood on a box to the left of the entrance to the security tower to allow my colleagues to search me for illegal substances. As they patted me down I noticed a temporary sign at the gate: 'No officer is allowed to leave Bank Kwang at this time. Please remain calm.' All prison rules were being followed to the letter that day. At 5am, 15 armed police left Phrapradaeng station in a van owned by the Royal Thai Police to pick up Sane at Samutprakarn Provincial Prison. A police car with siren blaring led the way.

Sane was probably the only one who didn't know he was about to die. I heard that he remained silent throughout the journey and mostly just gazed at his open palms, possibly trying to gauge his destiny from his life line. We Thais believe in fate and destiny. The life line is the line that extends from the edge of the palm above the thumb, and curves like a rainbow towards the wrist.

At 5.50am the van arrived at Bang Kwang Prison. Sane was now under the jurisdiction of the Execution Supervision Committee which was appointed by the Ministry of Interior. He was met at the prison entrance by the then prison Superintendent Slab Visutthimuk, Sompong Choomworathayee, Governor of Nonthaburi and prison doctor Dr Sujarit Pamornbood.

While the van was briefly delayed at the entrance a reporter ran to the window and asked a visibly surprised Sane if he had any last words for his family. The reporter repeated his question to which Sane smiled and replied: 'Tell my parents to come visit me'.

At 6am the prison Chaplain, Phra Mahasai Thanamangkaro, then abbot of the temple, arrived to perform Sane's last rites. Ten minutes later, Sane's fingerprints were taken for the execution records, and the Superintendent read the out the execution order to him. He exploded with rage and showered the prison staff with threats and expletives.

'I didn't fucking do it. I don't know a god damn thing about it. I will haunt you motherfuckers throughout all your lives. Let me see the face of the detective in charge! Where's the son of a bitch?'

The prison and police officers cowed under his fury and moved closer together. What if he was telling the truth and he was innocent? The detective who led the investigation assured us that that wasn't the case.

'Sane is not innocent. He has raped countless girls in his village. Most of his victims were afraid of his influential father so he thought he would get away scot free. He committed this particular crime with his kid brother; we have collected a substantial amount of evidence against him. The bastard won't make any more trouble for these people.'

His words calmed us officers while Sane continued to shout and scream obscenities at us. Without thinking I approached Sane and spoke quietly to him.

'Calm down. Stop shouting and pull yourself together. You can't do anything else at this point now.

Just think of it as bad karma coming back to you for what you have done. If you are positive when you 'go' you will end up in a good place, so empty your mind of anger and negativity.'

In Buddhism it is believed that if you are thinking positive when you die you will be born in to a good place in your next life. Sane refused to shut up completely, though he did simmer down a little.

At 6.30am he was offered papers and pencil to write his last will but he turned away saying, 'I'm not fucking doing it! I've got nothing to give anyone'.

After a couple of minutes he changed his mind and asked to write the following letter to his father;

> *Dear Dad,*
>
> *I just want to say goodbye to you. I hope you won't be too sad. Just think of it as a natural occurrence, we're bound to birth, age, be hurt and die anyway. Please look after my wife and don't let her struggle. Tell her not to take another husband. Don't bury my body, keep it for three years. Don't forget, Dad, to visit Narat as often as you can.*

When he was finished, the prison officers brought him to the Chaplain to hear the words of Buddha for one last time and ask for forgiveness. Sane refused to participate or sit on the floor. He was still furious and spat: 'No god can help me now. I was a monk. Don't waste my time. If you are going to kill me just do it!'

At 6.50am he was brought his last meal and reacted to that as he had to the Chaplain.

'I won't fucking eat it! You motherfuckers want to shoot me? Then go ahead and do it. Don't waste my time.'

It was decided to do as he wished and escort him to the execution room. Sane constantly urged the prison warders to take care of his younger brother. Then, a few steps down the hall he asked for a cigarette. I remember that moment as if it happened yesterday. He inhaled deeply without looking at any of us and continued walking purposely in his leg irons towards the door of the execution room, without pause or regret. It was said afterwards that the sound of his chains bashing together could be heard outside the prison. When he was asked to drop his cigarette he stubbornly stood to quickly finish it and then entered the room.

At exactly 7am, Sane was blindfolded and led to the cross to be secured to it. With his back to the gun, his arms were brought over the arms of a cross and tied together, as if in prayer, behind the horizontal beam. Sane tried to prevent his hands being placed in the wai, or praying, position, and fought against the bouquet of flowers being pushed between his palms. This practice meant that the condemned went to death with a last plea of forgiveness for his bad deeds. He was tied to the cross in two further places, around the torso and stomach and was pulled astride a bar that stuck out from the cross forcing him to hug the cross between his knees. His ankles were still chained together so the cross was now completely supporting him.

One last tug on the rope and he was ready. Behind him the screen was pulled across, separating him from the gun. There was a square white cloth on the screen with a concentric circle pinned on it which denoted the prisoner's heart—the target. Sawaeng Puangsookrak, the gun adjuster, aimed the gun for this white square and when he was satisfied he nodded to the executioner for that day, Mui Juijaroen. Mui was a thin, quiet man who enjoyed a drink. I didn't know him too well, I don't think anyone did. He kept mostly to himself. He had already experienced a small level of fame as a result of his job and had been interviewed by journalists a couple of times. He was the prison executioner from 1960-1974, and shot 48 criminals in that time.

I watched him step forward to the gun stand that looked for all the world like a sewing machine. He turned and saluted the Execution Supervision Committee as a sign of respect and then saluted Sane through the screen for his forgiveness before moving to bend over the gun, pressing his eye to the sight and moving his hand over the trigger.

He waited there, glancing neither right nor left. I wasn't even sure if he was breathing. The gun separated him from the rest of his colleagues. I cannot say that anyone looked at him enviously. In fact we probably experienced a collective shiver of fear as he appeared temporarily lost to us and utterly focused on what he had to do. The white cloth suddenly looked very small and vulnerable while the gun appeared to grow in size, demanding all our attention. Its ugliness seemed to suck all the warmth and energy out of the room. I felt that even if Mui wanted to walk away the machine wouldn't let him. It was too late now for anything other than what was to happen.

The head of the execution team took his position to the far right of the gun holding the red flag tensely in his hand. This flag normally stood in a pole attached to the wall when the room wasn't in use, the only colour in the room. Once the escorts had tied the prisoner to the cross and moved away the red flag is held high until the executioner signals that he is ready. At 7.11am the red flag was lowered and Mui pulled the trigger. One shot rang out that bright summer's morning with six bullets hitting Sane from the Bergmann submachine gun, followed by a shocked silence. Mui straightened up, turned his back to the screen and quickly left the room. The doctor entered the room immediately after, passing by the gun and then the screen to check on Sane. He felt for a pulse and then pushed up the blindfold to shine a torch into his eyes, searching for a reaction from the retinas. There was no sign of life and he confirmed that Sane was dead.

The bullets had penetrated his back and he stood almost as if he was sunk into a last embrace with the cross. His neck and head had fallen back as if he was looking skywards. The scene was grotesque. For six minutes after the shot a gurgling was heard from his corpse; the soul was taking its time leaving his body. Sane was protesting and defiant to the bitter end. The escorts untied him and lay him fast down on the ground. The blood seeped out of him on to the floor. I could also see blood on the cross and on a couple of the sand bags. His fingerprints had to be collected again to verify that the right guy had been executed.

Afterwards, Mui was interviewed by a newspaper and the journalist asked how he felt about Sane. He was definite in his reply.

'Over the last seven years I've seen more than a hundred convicts who have been sentenced to death but I have never seen such a mean and cruel felon like he was. No matter how much people kill, when they meet the Chaplain they pray and ask for forgiveness. Some are so upset they can't even stand when they hear the execution order and we have to put them in a wheelchair. Sane was an unapologetic bastard.'

CHAPTER 6

15 June 1972.

At 3.30pm Jumras Janopas, the Commander of Wing 1 at Bang Kwang, had three convicts brought to the Security Tower for their execution. They had all been sentenced to death by the Supreme Court in 1971. They had appealed to have the death sentence overturned and then had to wait nine months to hear that their appeals had been rejected because of the severity of their crimes. This was faster than the norm, which was usually a 12 month wait.

This was my first time to be an escort. I hadn't been expecting to play a part in the proceedings. My boss, Prayad Loharatana, the head of the custody section, had sent for me at 6am that morning. I wondered if I was in trouble and hurried over to his office. I quickly checked to see if my uniform was neat and knocked on his door. He bid me come in and close the door.

'Chavoret we have one today. Could you be the escort? We're short of staff.'

I stared at him.

'But sir I don't know how to be an escort. I've never done it before.'

He shrugged impatiently saying 'There's nothing to it. Just walk behind the older guys and do what they do. Look we're really short of staff, are you going to help me or not?'

I had made an impression on my superiors by trying to calm Sane down. At the time I thought that I had simply reacted instinctively to an angry man in distress. However, with hindsight I wonder if I was showing off again. I would never lick up to a boss or kiss ass. I don't believe it is necessary if you can prove that you are a good steady worker with initiative.

I felt I was being tested to see if I would rise to a challenge. I had never believed myself to be particularly good at anything. I had done alright at school but not enough to be a teacher. I played the guitar in plenty of bands but never excelled as a musician. I knew a bit about medicine but not enough to be a doctor. Being part of the execution was a serious undertaking. I had heard that some prison officers had fainted at their first execution. But it was also a career move, a reflection that my boss saw potential in me and felt he could trust me with more duties. How many people turn down their bosses when they are personally complimented for their daily performance with an opportunity to take on more responsibility? I looked my chief in the eye and said yes.

Being an escort can be a tricky business. It's probably one of the most emotional roles in the whole process of execution because you personally pick up the prisoner from his cell. In other words, you are death's messenger. Then you can end up spending a lot of time with the prisoner before he dies. When it is time the escort brings the condemned into the execution room and ties him to the cross. After the prisoner has been confirmed dead by the doctor it is the escort who unties him and lays him down on the floor. Even the executioner does not have to see the body after he has done his job.

The other officers and I went in to Wing 1 to pick up the prisoners. As usual there was a tension in the air as the other death row prisoners wondered if they were to be collected too. It was a bleak day outside with dark clouds almost falling out of the sky under a weight of gloom. I cannot pretend that it is an easy thing to do, to make that walk with my colleagues past frightened faces until we reach the ones whose time has run out. The first two that we picked up looked at us in sheer panic when we stopped outside their cell. They knew that something was up because earlier they had been put in the same cell—partners-in-crime were never locked up together. We let them say their goodbyes to the other inmates who looked stricken on their behalf.

**

By this time, I had made a point of finding out more about the prisoners doomed to die. This case was pretty awful. Somsak Patan and 'Piek' Twat Sutakul had happened upon Supapun Ratanataya, a young librarian from Thammasart University, who was visiting Sammuk Mountain in the province of Chonburi with her boyfriend. The couple was set upon by these experienced and hardened men. First Supapun's boyfriend was forced to watch her being raped by the two men. Then Supapun had to watch her boyfriend being killed before she too was finally murdered. The case was well-known and had shocked the country with its brutality. But this wasn't the reason for their execution; they had committed plenty of murders before this.

The third convict to be executed that day was 34-year-old Jaroen Yimlamul who had murdered a farmer in Lopburi Province and stolen all his livestock of cows and buffaloes. He had also killed before.

There was a very official reception waiting for the men in the security tower. They were met by the prison's Superintendent Slab Visutthimuk, the head of the prison hospital, Sujarit Phamornbutr, the Inspector of the Department of Corrections, Prasert Mekmanee, head of the vocational training centre; Prayad Loharat, chief of the custody section, and lastly there was a guy representing the Governor of Nonthaburi.

At 3.45pm their fingerprints were taken for the records and their last meals were placed in front of them. All three dinners of soup, fruit and dessert remained untouched. This was typical. I can't imagine that I would want to eat a few minutes before I was going to be executed, though the meal was a lot better than the normal fare suffered by the prisoners. The Chaplain Phramahasai read some Buddhist teachings to them. Somasak was Islamic so he washed his feet, face and hands and then knelt down to say his own prayers. They were then offered pencils and paper to write to their families. Jareon refused to write anything. He chain smoked while the other two accepted the stationery and briefly thought about what they wanted to say.

Somak wrote to his mother and youngest brother to tell them they were always in his thoughts. He also asked them to pick up his body with 24 hours of his death as keeping with his faith—the prison had a special arrangement with an Islamic organization and ensured that the convicts' and families' wishes were carried out. His faith also prevented him from donating any body parts unlike Piek who was donating his eyes to the Thai Red Cross and his body to the Faculty of Medicine at Siriraj. Consequently his note was to tell his family not to collect his body. Doctor Sujarit Pamornbood had campaigned for and instigated this practice but after receiving a huge amount of criticism the prison authorities decided to discontinue it shortly afterwards. It didn't seem appropriate to be asking someone to make a donation of their organs when they were trying to cope and prepare themselves for their imminent death.

After that all they could do was wait. By then Piek had banished his fears and was in exceptionally good form. He laughed and joked with the prison officers.

He answered all questions put to him, confirming that he had actually killed 27 people. He challenged the other two to see if they could beat that figure. However, Somak admitted to killing only nine and Jareon admitted to four murders. Then Piek went one better and sang to the officers 'Rak Jak Daungjai' (Love From My Heart).

At 4.30pm Jareon was placed in the wooden cart to make the journey from the tower to the execution room. This cart was more like a wheelbarrow with a chair propped up on it. Mui was still the executioner then. He fired the Bergmann gun which sent five bullets into the back of Jareon's heart, killing him instantly. At 5pm it was Somsak's turn and he was wheeled off to a similar fate. Piek never looked frightened or troubled, even when Somsak was taken away. He continued to chat as if he hadn't a care in the world. Finally at 5.30pm I got him into the cart. As I pushed him down the path he burst into song again, singing 'Pee Boon Noi' (I'm Unlucky) to us officers. One of the officers asked Piek if he would appear to him in a dream and give him the lottery numbers. This is a Thai belief; when someone you know dies they can visit you in your dreams and pass on useful information like the lotto numbers which is a serious business in Thailand.

There are all sorts of monks and gurus who claim they can help you with lotto numbers and as a result they can count big gamblers among their many followers.

Piek told my colleague that he would help him out in exchange for the officer making a merit for him. The prisoner waved gaily at all he passed and just before I pushed him into the room he asked us all to look after his friends who were serving life sentences—we were to give his mattress to Jare his cell-mate. Like the two before him, five bullets were used to kill him. He had amazed me with his attitude. His execution was probably the easiest that I had ever been involved with. It was the only time that I asked a condemned man if he really did commit the crimes he was charged with, which proves how relaxed he looked to me. I felt that he knew his chosen life style was always going to bring him to this point, and so here it was—pay-back time. He had become addicted to playing god with other peoples' lives but it was always going to end badly for him. He was happy to go; it was only fair after all he had gotten away with. But don't get me wrong, I didn't admire him for it.

Both Piek and Somsak were only 26 years old when they were executed. They could have lived their lives differently and make their parents proud. I didn't feel sorry for them, they had committed terrible crimes—36 people were dead because of them. What they did to that poor librarian and her boyfriend was horrific. They were pure evil. I believe there are truly bad people who can never be cured of their desire to do depraved things. I don't think prison will make them any better than they are, and yes, I believe this type of person deserves to die.

CHAPTER 7

My career went from strength to strength and soon I had become an experienced officer. I had seen death up close, and learned to deal with it, how best to help carry out the cold and calculated executions. It was the way to get the job done. I didn't think about the condemned that much, and I didn't pity them. They were just as cold and pitiless when they took the lives of the innocent.

31 May 1972.

The bus-stop in front of the Olympia building on Rama IV Road, Bangkok.

The number 76 bus stopped and there was the hustle and bustle of people getting off and on. Three men watched one well-dressed woman laden down with bags as she jostled to get on the bus. Sanong Phobang slipped his hand into her handbag and tried to grab some money. As she was about to step on to the bus, two men, Thanoochai Montriwat and Jumnian Jantra, pressed against her on either side. Jumnian nodded at Sanong Phobang, who proceeded, from behind, to open up one of her other bags. Suddenly a male passenger shouted from the bus;

'You're being pick pocketed,' and pointed to Sanong. The three men were furious and Sanong roared at the other two:

'GET HIM!'

Jumnian attempted to climb up the window of the bus but the driver had started to accelerate away from the stop. Unfortunately the three men were able to jump on the back and charged upstairs. The bus stopped 200 metres down the road at the Sala Daeng Junction. Jumnian ran to the front of the bus to prevent the passenger, Boonyarid, from getting off. Sanong followed him and then removed a small knife from Jumnian's back pocket. He brandished the knife over the heads of the frightened passengers as he closed in on Boonyarid who sat petrified in his seat. Then, understandably, it got too much for him and he decided to make a run for it. With his eyes on the knife in Sanong's hand he raced to the front where he was duly grabbed by Jumnian who held him by the collar, allowing Sanong to stab him once in the chest. Even as Boonyarid was falling to the ground the three men had jumped off the bus and ran, not one passenger hampering their escape in any way.

Thanks to the amount of witnesses the three men were arrested within a fortnight, over three consecutive days. Jumnian, Thanoochai (or Daengyik) and Sanong were caught respectively on the 8, 9 and 10 June. They confessed that they and other groups had targeted bus passengers as they got on or off a bus, and they also admitted to beating up, even killing, anyone who told on them.

While they were being investigated in custody two passengers from another bus came forward with fresh allegations. At 6pm, 28 April 1972, the three suspects had been on the number 18 bus attempting to pick pocket a Thai-Chinese woman. Her husband, Sanan, spotted what they were up to and gently chided them saying, 'Brothers you can't do this.' Again the robbers responded with rage. Sanan had been standing downstairs with his wife near the door. One of the men grabbed him by the shirt and dragged him off the bus and on to the road side where they all started to thrash him. Somehow Sanan managed to get to his feet and started running down the street with the three in angry pursuit. He hadn't got a chance—they soon caught up with him and stabbed him. He collapsed and died in front of a restaurant near Soi Phayanark.

Thongyoo Gerddee was on the bus and witnessed the whole episode while Prom Yimprasert told the police that she recognized the three as soon as she saw their photographs in the newspaper. They had been standing with her and her husband at the bus-stop before the number 18 appeared.

The three men denied murdering Sanan. Jumnian did admit that he had been previously arrested and charged with stealing and assault. Thanoochai admitted that he had served a prison sentence of one year and four months for stealing and knowingly buying stolen goods. Sanong admitted that he had been previously arresting for stealing. However, all of this confessing did not save them. The prison received a summary execution order from General Thanom Kittikajorn on 19 June which said that their repeat offences showed the men to be inordinately cruel and beyond respecting the law, therefore they must be punished by execution. That was how I got to know them.

The men were being held at Lumpini station and the police there had them on suicide watch. They were each in a cell of their own with their own officer who stayed with them 24 hours. They were allowed no contact with the world outside before the announcement— no visitors, no newspapers and no pencil and paper. They kidded with one another, flicking rubber bands through their bars.

Sanong grew cocky and told the police man who was guarding him; 'Since we are about to leave here I want to level with you bro. I have pick pocketed over a hundred times.' The guard replied by asking him how many men he had killed. Sanong's face darkened and he ignored the question. He turned away from the guard and said: 'The worse case scenario is that I'll be jailed for 20 years, but if I behave and receive a pardon I'll be out in no time.'

At noon on the day of the execution a crowd gathered outside the police station. The officers were distracted with trying to keep order, which allowed Sanong's wife, Somkid Lareuang, and her aunt Jumpee Chanamit to sneak in to find Sanong in his cell. Sanong was agitated when he saw them. The three prisoners could hear the crowd and the noise and it made them nervous. Sanong asked them what was going on outside. Jumpee told him that it was just some people having trouble with the police. He told his aunt to help Somkid bring up their son and give him a good education. They were interrupted by an officer who ordered the women to leave the station. Jumpee broke down in tears and had to be helped out by her niece. Sanong called after them not to worry, that a 20 year sentence was the worst that could happen.

A few hours later, at 3pm, officers marched into the three cells and handcuffed the men before escorting them outside to three separate police cars. The men looked visibly frightened now and Thanoochai's voice shook as he asked an officer where they were being taken to. The officer refused to answer him or even look at him, which told the men all they needed to know. They paled and Jumnian's legs went from under him. He and the others were held up by their arms and led out to the cars. There were six police officers for each prisoner and car. The leading car in the convoy sounded its siren while police jeeps brought up the rear.

At 3.30pm the convoy stopped at Wat Larnboonna Junction on Ngamwongwan Road. The car that held Jumnian had broken down. Jumnian had also fainted again and had to be carried to another car. He fainted again in the five minutes that it took to reach the prison. At 3.35pm the convoy reached the prison gates. Superintendent Slab Visutthimuk ordered the execution team to make the necessary preparations. Mui had already left for his dormitory and had to be quickly summoned back. The prison had provided him with a room and it wasn't too far away. At 3.40pm the prisoners were escorted by police officers and prison staff to the security tower. They were joined there by the Chaplain who read them Buddha's words. Sanong, who was Islamic, asked the monk to do an Islamic ritual while Thanoonchai and Jumnian looked on miserably.

An officer brought them three glasses of iced water which the men ignored. After the Chaplain had finished the prisoners were offered paper and pencils to write to their families. Juminian wrote:

'Don't follow in my footsteps. I have to pay now for all that I have done. I hope you stay well and happy.'

Thanoonchai wrote to his mother: 'I didn't know what was happening. I wish I could see you now. Please take care of my children and my wife.'

Sanong wrote one line to his family: 'Goodbye, I have to pay for my sins now.'

The Superintendent read out the summary execution to the seated men. Suddenly it hit the three of them that this was it. Thanoochai fell out of his chair and screamed for mercy.

'Please don't kill me sir. Let me see my mother first, she knows people, let her help me, please let me see her!'

The prisoners hugged each other and cried like children.

Mui cycled into the prison at 3.50pm and headed to the execution room to check on the gun. Finally at 5.25pm the other escort and myself led Jumnian out of the tower and over to the execution room. Nobody spoke. I think I half expected him to faint but he didn't. He had resigned himself to his fate and was like 'a dead man walking'. We had blindfolded him at the gazebo and when we reached the room we firmly secured him to the cross. The screen was pulled forward, and the gun adjuster, Sawaeng Puangsoodrak, stepped back from the gun to let Mui take his place. Mui readied himself over the Bergmann and waited for the flag to drop. He fired one shot, which sent eight bullets into Jumnian's back. He died instantly.

I headed back with the other escort to collect Thanoochai. He blanched when he saw us but didn't try to resist as we brought him out of the tower. However, all hell broke out at the execution room. He shocked me by suddenly tearing off the blindfold and shouting out for his mother. He kept insisting that his mother be allowed to see him as she could save him because of who she knows, and implored us not to kill him. All the time he was shouting his pleas his eyes roved around wildly searching for his mother but of course she wasn't there. She was probably in her kitchen praying for him. The staff just stood there staring at him in horror. He really seemed to think his mother was going to appear and save him.

Then he remembered his friend who had gone before him and began to call out for Jumnian.

'Nian! Are you in there? Answer me man. Do you hear me? Answer me you asshole. Are you dead? Why don't you answer me?'

The silence was almost cruel, as if he was being taunted in his madness on top of everything else. I briefly wondered if some fool had told him something to get his hopes up—just tell the officers that your mother knows some government official and they will have to stop the execution. A split second passed and Thanoochai realised that Jumnian would never reply to his shouts, followed by the realisation that it was also too late for him. He crumpled to the floor in front of the execution room, surrounded by staff, and began to cry quietly. I had to do something. I signalled the other escort and we helped him to his feet. All his fight had gone now, but he still had not lost hope. As we half dragged, half carried him into the room, he still called out for his mother;

'Please help me Mom, please help me.'

It was tough to witness, but we had a job to do, with another execution still to be done. That was all I could allow myself to think about—we had orders and orders have to be obeyed. Also I was very aware that we were being watched by our superiors and their superiors. Thanoochai started to struggle when we got to the cross and I had to think quickly. It would be better for all of us, not least of all him, to get this over with as fast as possible. I grabbed my handkerchief out of my back pocket and shoved it into his mouth. I didn't want add further to his or our distress so I didn't want to put him in a head lock or handcuff him. He became enraged and fell to the floor once more, rolling around trying to dodge us. It took four of us to get him standing in front of the cross again. Then I pushed my knee into his back to force him against the cross so that we could bind him to it. One guy tied his hands up around the cross; another guy tied his weight while the other escort and I tried to stop his squirming. Only when he was completely secure did he finally shut up.

At 5.40pm Mui fired 12 bullets into Thanoochai.

I was glad to be able to leave the room with the other guard to pick up Sanong. The couple of seconds of fresh air was like a balm to my aching head. Sanong didn't give us any trouble at all. He walked obediently into the execution room, his head bowed by the guilt for his past actions. He didn't acknowledge anyone or look for sympathy. It took just seconds to tie him to the cross. He died at 5.57pm from 12 bullets.

By the time Sanong's body had been removed to the morgue, the room stank of blood, sweat and gun powder. There was a lot of blood from each of the men all over the floor and the sand bags. Unfortunately the floor is never cleaned immediately after a shooting. Sand is just thrown down to blot up the puddles and left there overnight for the inmates, who are in charge of the room, to tidy up the following morning.

***

We were all emotionally drained and were more than glad when our shift was over that day. To alleviate tension, or guilt, a few of us went for a drink afterwards. Mui, as usual, was long gone. He always left immediately after the prisoner was confirmed dead. Thanoochai's outburst dominated the conversation. We agreed that his reaction was completely understandable and natural—everyone is afraid of dying. Some of the men wondered why we didn't see more convicts crack up in the execution room. After a while we moved on to other things. Some of the men believed the execution room to be full of ghosts. More than once officers had gone in to investigate noises or were convinced that there were a couple of people walking around the room, only to find it empty. One of the guys needed to grab forty winks a while back and had sat down to take a nap outside the room. He slept soundly until he was woken up by someone, who wasn't there.

Early the following morning Thanoochai's mother arrived to pick up her son's body. She asked to see the head of the custody section, Prayad Loharatana. She told him that her son appeared in her dreams the previous night and told her that he had lost his shoes. The chief summoned me and told me to take care of her. She was trembling and pale and I asked her how I could help her.

She replied: 'Officer, I dreamt about my son last night. He was crying and when I asked him why he didn't answer. He just stood there and then blood started to ooze out of every part of his body.'

She broke down and sobbed at this and I just kept patting her on the arm until she was able to speak again.

'He told me he lost his shoes and asked me to get them back. He just kept repeating that. I don't really understand but I'm afraid he won't be able to rest in peace, which is why I need your help.'

I assured her that I would help in any way that I could and that I would be in touch. I asked the inmates who were in charge of removing the shackles from the prisoners after death, cleaning the body and putting it into the coffin. The bodies were kept in the Buddhist temple where they were collected by the relatives. Sure enough, Mhong, a former undertaker, saw Thanoochai's shoes and fancied them for himself. Since Thanoochai wasn't an inmate of Bang Kwang his shoes were much nicer and in better condition. Normally the dead inmates' shoes would just be discarded but Mhong thought that would be a terrible waste. He took them, cleaned them thoroughly and left them out to dry in the sun.

That afternoon Thanoochai's mother left with her son's body, including his newly washed shoes. She was a good woman and kept begging her son's victims to see into their hearts if they could forgive her son. She was going to cremate the body and wanted Thanoochai to feel in the consuming flames, the goodness and forgiveness emanating from everyone he had hurt which would fill him with regret and sorrow for his criminal ways. A parent's love can be the purest love there is; no matter what a child does he is forgiven and still fiercely loved.

***

It troubles me still that I was driven to stuffing that handkerchief into Thanoochai's mouth but I don't think there was anything else I could have done. It had the desired effect of stifling his wrath, which allowed us to tie him to the cross. Once the prisoner is firmly secured he usually goes quiet. My priority was to speed up the process—the longer it took the more worked up he became. Also it is not fair to increase the stress of an already tense execution team. The situation is bad enough and no one takes their duty lightly. We are not proud to be involved in the ending of someone's life— it is simply part of our job. The prison had received a summary execution order from the government about these three men and we were told to carry it out immediately.

The summary execution order no longer happens in Thailand. Nowadays the prisoner has a chance to fight his case in court and prove his innocence to a jury. Even when it did, during the rule of General Thanom, the government only got involved in cases that had particularly shocked the nation or threatened national security. The two murdered husbands I mentioned, Sanan and Boonyarid, had done no harm to anyone. They had merely called attention to pick pockets and for this they lost their lives in the most cowardly and callous fashion.

***

On 20 June 1972, the day after the men had been executed, journalists from *Thairath*, the big Thai newspaper, went to interview Boonyarid's parents. His father had left for work but his mother told them that they were both glad that the government had acted speedily in punishing the killers. The family had received hundreds of letters of condolences, including one from General Thanom himself.

Prom, Sanan's wife, received lots of donations in the post to make up for the loss of her husband. She was also glad that the killers had been dealt with so efficiently. She had worried that they would not be punished at all. However, she did say that she would pray for the three men and send her forgiveness to them.

An eye for an eye—Personally, I think that's the way it should be. There are some people who will never see the error of their ways; who would not benefit from years in prison, they would go back out into the world and kill again. The death penalty is not the perfect solution but I cannot think of a perfect alternative. Some people are just evil to the core. As you can see from the reactions of Boonyarid's and Sanan's families' people want the murderers of their relatives to pay the ultimate price, the same one that their loved one had paid. I remember once being asked by a victim's mother if she could shoot the guy herself. Is this just a Thai thing?

CHAPTER 8

Not all of the inmates sentenced to death were common criminals or murderers, and I found myself at times involved in the execution of people caught up in political causes, but as part of terrorist groups, or even involving corruption within the State. In the end though, if they killed innocent people, they usually found themselves up in front of me.

On 28 January 1977, in the Aranyapratade District of Prajeenburi Province, police officers arrested five men; Mun Boonprasert, Thianchai Thongyoo, Somjai Jantra, Yoo Jark and Suheng Saekoo. They had led a group of Cambodian soldiers to attack three defenceless Thai villages and burn them to the ground. 28 Thais lost their lives. It was all part of a big criminal operation involving corrupt police and customs officers. Guns, bullets and explosive devices had been smuggled out to Cambodian soldiers, along with top secret information about the Thai Army, and also to a terrorist group in the Wattananakorn District. Illegal substances and stolen goods were also being exported out of the country.

The arrests were the result of a lot of investigation and patience on the part of the police. This was a serious breach of trust by those in uniform. Not surprisingly, a summary execution order was issued by the Prime Minister Thanin Kraivichian on 13 June 1977. The following is an excerpt:

'These men are a threat to national security and have sabotaged peace among Thai citizens. Therefore it is necessary to act quickly and confront this threat for the sake of our peaceful society. Guided by Section 21 of the Constitution, and with the approval of the Cabinet and Council, the Prime Minister orders that the following men be punished by execution; Mun Boonprasert, Yoo Jark, Somjai Jantra. Suheng Saekoo is sentenced to life imprisonment. Since 15-year-old Thianchai Thongyoo is a juvenile, and has co-operated with the police in custody he is to be shown leniency and imprisoned for just five years. The Ministry of Interior must deliver this order immediately.'

That meant it was time for my team to go to work. At 10.30pm, 13 June, the Governor of Prajeenburi, Direk Sodsatid, summoned Han Pansomboon, then Superintendent of Bang Kwang, and Chaleaw Sithiprasert, then Superintendent of Prajeenburi Provincial Prison. After a brief meeting they decided that the executions would take place in the Kabinburi district prison. The police were informed and they contacted the soldiers holding the convicts in a camp in Aranyapratade District with instructions to bring them to Kabinburi. However, the Governor was then informed by officers who had reached the district prison that it wasn't suitable for the executions; it lacked the adequate space required. The decision was quickly taken to use the prison in Prajeenburi instead.

The following morning almost 100 officers guarded the new location and were kept busy dispersing the crowds that tried to gather at the front of the prison. As usual they were not going to be permitted to witness the execution so they did the next best thing and handed their cameras to the police, imploring them to take pictures for them. At 2.50am the Bang Kwang execution team arrived in two vans at Prajeenburi.

This included the Superintendent, Songwut Arsachai, who was heading the team and would perform the flag duties; the executioner Prathom Kruepeng, and me, in my new role as the gun adjuster. We had all travelled together from Bang Kwang and it felt like a road-trip. The journey took six hours, having left Bang Kwang at approximately 9pm and making several food stops. The conversation ran from general topics to going over the details of the execution; it was crucial that everything went smoothly since this was our first job away from home, and we were representing our prison. We were brought to where the execution would take place outside—at the back wall of the building, near a pond. About an hour later the Chaplain, Phrakroovijid Suphasunggarn, arrived to perform the last rites. He was followed a short while later by the convoy of police and soldiers who were escorting the three condemned men.

While I was still an escort I had shown an interest in the gun itself. I always like to know how things work; even now, I don't understand why people my age are not computer literate. My generation tends to shy away from such things, even touching them, reckoning they have lasted long enough without using one, whereas I signed up for courses and am quite proud today of my skills. So it was with the equipment at work. After one execution, a while ago, I had passed by the room in order to deliver some papers and spied Sawaeng inside cleaning the gun. I wandered in and found myself helping him. I think he was touched by my interest and took the time to teach me about all the different parts—how to load it, lock it and clean it. He was the one who emphasized to me how the onus to ensure a speedy death for the prisoner, lay squarely on the shoulders of the guy who adjusts the gun and lines it up for the shooter. He started to let me clean the gun after a shooting and gradually the machine was as familiar to me as it was to him. So it was a natural progression when Sawaeng reached retirement that my name was put forward to take his place. Knowledge is power and I always urge my kids to learn, learn, learn.

***

At 5am the registrar, Jaran Prasong-ngern, and the official photographer, Prasit Gongpermpul, commenced their duties. Finger prints and photos were taken of the convicts for police records. Then the execution order was read to them. They made no response as they listened and then signed their name to it. They were offered pens and papers but refused them, explaining to the officers that they had no possessions to leave to anyone. At 5.15am they sat on the floor and listened to the monk perform his absolutions. I was told that Mun Booprasert had already broken down once, screaming in fear and panic, but the escorts managed to calm him down and now he looked as impassive as his two friends. The escorts had given the men 50 baht each so that they could make their last merit with the Chaplain and ask for forgiveness.

At 5.40am two escorts carried Mun to the cross first. He was firmly secured and the screen with the target depicted on it was pulled across. I walked to the gun and pointed it squarely at the white square. I loaded 15 bullets into it; 15 was the required amount to put in per person but rarely would they all be needed. I turned back the wheel of the gun stand to lock the gun in position and then stepped away to the side. Prathom took his place over the gun and waited for the flag to be lowered. Nine bullets were fired into Mun, who died instantly. The doctor checked his pulse and retinas, and confirmed him to be dead as Prathom moved away and I retrieved the gun's magazine and counted how many bullets had been used.

At 6.10am the second man, Yoo, wished his friend good luck and bid him goodbye. The escorts brought him out, leaving a much stressed Somjai behind. He asked his escort for a cigarette and his hand trembled as he took it. As he smoked the tears began to flow.

'I'm innocent sir, I really am. A police man's son did this, not me, but the police beat me so badly that I had to sign the confession. I deliver oil, that's all I do. I didn't know anything about it, you must believe me.'

At 6.20am Prathom saluted Yoo and pulled the trigger, and six bullets took the criminal's life. It was now Somjai's turn. As he was brought to the cross he cried out to everyone;

'I'm innocent. I'm no weapon smuggler—I deliver oil for a living. I had nothing to do with any of this.'

His escort blindfolded him and tied him quickly to cross. Yoo was upset but he didn't put up a struggle. When the screen was pulled across I walked to the gun to load it and put it in position. But something was wrong. I had put the 15 bullets in but I couldn't unlock the gun to move it. It was stuck. I stared at the machine in bewilderment. Ampan Janjui, my Bang Kwang colleague who was a gun expert, appeared beside me but he couldn't get the gun to move either.

Our Superintendent hissed at us to use the spare gun that we had brought with us. It had already been assembled just in case we needed it. I quickly loaded 15 bullets into it and went to unlock it. It was stuck too. I could not believe it. Ampan and I looked at one another as the onlookers gasped and began to murmur their incredulity. Some of the officers thought it must be a supernatural power sending a sign; I just thought there was something wrong with the gun. I lifted if from the stand and carefully examined it. I could find absolutely nothing wrong. I had expected to find a bullet stuck but no, everything was fine. Now what?

Suddenly Dokrung Wongnarong, an experienced escort, had an idea and went back to Somjai to search him thoroughly. He found a relic of a famous Buddhist monk hidden in Somjai's right armpit. In Thailand you can buy relics or protective charms from the likes of spirit doctors, trance mediums and monks. 'Phra Khreuang' are Buddha pendants or portraits of famous monks.

'What is this coin, lil' bro? Where did you get it?'

Somjai replied that it was 'Luangpho Daeng's coin sir, my mother gave it to me.'

Dokrung saluted the sky and cut the rope that tied the coin to Somjai's arm. He brought the relic over to the Execution Supervision Committee.

I tried to unlock the gun again. I aimed the gun away and pulled the lever. One shot was fired. I placed the gun back on the stand and adjusted it. Prathom took over from me. He saluted Somjai and fired the gun. Nine bullets were fired. The escorts untied his body. The fingerprints of the three men were taken again, and then the bodies were cleaned and put aside for the families to collect them. But nobody turned up to claim them. Police officers explained to me later that the three families were Cambodian and lived in Thailand, and they were probably too afraid to come pick them up.

After the work was done, the staff at Prajeenburi treated us very well and laid on a meal for us: tom yum koong and spicy salads. I was proud to be sharing a table with my superiors and really felt like I was an important and appreciated member of a team.

Later in Bang Kwang the gun sticking caused concern and there was a meeting of the 'suits'. It was decided that our equipment needed to be updated. Noppakoon Tanutis was a gun expert who wrote a column for the *Ban Muang* newspaper. He and Tawee

Choosap, Vice Director of DOC, made the crucial decision about what would replace our old gun. The Bergmann MP 34/1 with a size nine parabellum had served us well from 1935 to 1984. Our new gun was to be the HK MP-5 9 parabellum with a silencer and this was the last gun to be used until 2003, when lethal injection would become the instrument of execution. Furthermore I was one of three officers who were appointed to receive the new gun and learn how to use it at the Armed Forces Security Centre. At least the silencer would offer a little mercy to the guy waiting his turn. The Bergmann was very loud, and the bang usually freaked out the second guy if there was more than one execution. Now I could even check the gun was properly aimed by trying it out a couple of hours before the execution took place, something that I could never have done with the blasted Bergmann, unless I wanted to cause a riot.

CHAPTER 9

I had now been in the job for several years, and had heard stories and reports of events that would turn even the strongest stomach. But the levels to which some people went, and the crimes they were capable of committing, never ceased to amaze me.

18 October 1978.

Bangrak Police Station in the district of Pathumwan.

Vichai Srijareonsukying and his wife Jitra, owners of the popular Somboonpochana Restaurant, are filing charges against their former employee, Ginggaew Lorsoongnern, and two accomplices, for the kidnapping of their six-year-old-son. Ginggaew had been their domestic cleaner and the child's nanny. They became more and dissatisfied with her work until

144

Above: I think my father spoilt me a little. I always had more toys than my friends, including my cowboy-style shooter. I got to use a very different type of gun years later.
Right: My father, who gave me everything I could ask for. He was a teacher, and for a while I wanted to be one too, before I discovered the guitar.

All images © Author's private collection

Above: My brother, Oud, on the left, and myself as young boys.
Below: I didn't have a sheltered upbringing. We lived between
the wealthy and the poor, with the slum, brothels and opium
dens at on end of the street and the big houses and gardens of
the well-to-do at the other.

I had a great time playing with various bands and being paid for the first time. A lot of the time our audience was made up of American soldiers taking a break from the war in Vietnam, and with my good English I made a lot of friends.

Above: Things were going really well when I started playing for the Mitra band at the Sorry About That Bar, a former skating rink. In the end my musical career was finished when I was called up to do my military service.

Below: Posing for a photograph in my military uniform.

Three sites you should hope you never see in your life; the 7-storey security tower at Bang Kwang (**Above**), a symbol of incarceration; the iron gates that close you in (**Right**), and the Execution Room (**Below**).

Above: Taking aim through the gun used to carry out executions, the HK MP5 submachine gun. 15 bullets are required per person, but rarely are they all needed. Officials and guests can view the event from behind the glass partition.

Above: Standing to attention beside my gun. It looks a little like a sewing machine, but there is no mistaking its purpose.

Above: I have always tried to treat the inmates like equals and sometimes put on gigs for their entertainment.

Above: Many people were surprised when I joined a religious order after I carried out my last execution.

Above: I am proud of my career and what I have achieved. I tried to make something good out of my years of executing people by talking to university and school students about how bad things can get if you are arrested and sentenced to Bang Kwang. If I can persuade one person not to commit a crime, then it is well worth it.

they eventually sacked her. A little while later she had turned up to collect the son from his school, one of her former duties, and brought him to Nakhon Ratchasrima province. He was probably delighted to see his nanny again and trotted off with her quite happily. Just before she collected him she had sent the ransom letter to his parents explaining what was happening and what was expected of them.

The couple was instructed to board a train and drop a paper bag containing the ransom money, 200,000 baht, at a designated spot between Pakchong and Jantuek train stations. The boy would be returned to them once they had the money. The kidnappers had marked the spot by putting a flag in the ground. Police officers accompanied the anxious parents with their bag of cash on to the train and they prepared to make the drop. Unfortunately it was a particularly dark night and the parents were quite naturally in a fragile state. As a result, they never saw the flag—and the money remained undelivered by the time they reached the end of the track.

The kidnappers, were anxious too, and desperate. They watched in disbelief as the train passed by the flag with nothing thrown from a window. Was this some sort of joke? Did they want their kid back or not?

The men exploded in fury, reckoning that the parents were being advised by the police not to hand over the money. Looking for an outlet to vent their anger, they found one in the sleeping child beside them. Without a word a knife was plunged into his neck and torso. The woman screamed in horror and tried to throw herself over the little boy to prevent him being stabbed again but she was viciously pulled off him and physically kicked out of the way. There was nothing she could do, there were too many of them. She lay hurt and sobbing as the men dragged the boy off into the darkness to some farmland nearby. She discovered later that the child's grave had already been dug, just in case.

Later, the coroner would report that soil was found in the child's lung—he had been buried alive. He was lying on his side, two feet beneath the ground, with a bunch of flowers, incense sticks and one candle shoved between his hands. His hands had been tied with saisin, which is sacred white thread used by monks in a variety of holy rituals. Thais believe that the thread wards off ghosts or evil spirits and monks are usually invited to house warming parties to drape saisin around the rooms to repel any lingering evil spirits. The killers did not want to be haunted by the child's spirit and were taking every precaution. Even later the woman,

Ginggaew, would claim she heard him cry out for his mother from beneath the ground.

In time the police arrested six people, one woman and five men: Ginggaew Lorsoungnern, Gasem Singhara, Pin Peungyard, Thongmuan Grogkoggraud, Thongsuk Puvised and Suthi Sridee. Three months later, on 12 January 1979, at 8pm, the following order was issued; Ginggaew, Gasem and Pin were to be executed; Thongsuk was sentenced to life imprisonment; Thongsuk who was married to Pin, and Suthi, were sentenced to 20 years imprisonment.

The first female executed by gun was Yai Sonthibumroong, who was shot at Bang Kwang on 25 February 1942, by Rhien Permgamlungmuang. Over 30 years later, Ginggaew was to be only the second woman to die this way. She would be the first woman that I would see executed, and she is the one that I will never forget for as long as I live.

On 13 January 1979, at 10.50am, the Superintendent of Klong Prem Prison, Prasarn Prasertprasart, and 15 armed officers brought Pin and Gasem in a convoy of three police cars to Bang Kwang. I was expecting their arrival. Each prisoner had four escorts assigned to him. The two men looked pathetic and miserable in their grimy prison uniforms. At the gates of Bang Kwang the cars were besieged by a small army of journalists and photographers desperate for information. The men shuddered in terror but were spared having to do any interviews as the gates opened, allowing only the police cars entrance. Once the two men were dispatched the same convoy left again for Lard Yao Women's Prison to make their final pick-up.

She arrived at Bang Kwang at 11.25am, closely guarded by the director of the female prison and prison officers. Bang Kwang's Superintendent, Tawil Na Taguatoong, and his staff were waiting to receive her in the Custody Office. She wore a long sleeved blouse and a simple skirt, and she looked absolutely terrified. There was a frenzy at the gates with journalists trying to get her attention, but the car swept past them.

Exaggerated and conflicting stories had made it into the papers, each one more dramatic than the other. She was all over the news, like some kind of film star. One paper added to the melodrama by describing how one of the men grabbed Ginggaew's hand and forced her, with some slaps to her face, to stab the sleeping child. In one account the boy was strangled by Pin, who then hit the dying boy in the back of the neck with a steel pipe. Another paper quoted Ginggaew saying that Pin first stabbed the boy, and because he wasn't dying quickly enough for the heartless man, grabbed the child and broke his neck. This paper described the child being found in the shallow grave with his head turned back to front. Very little of it could have been true, or even known. But certainly, none of it made easy reading, especially for young parents.

I remember that day so clearly. At 3pm a prison guard was sent to fetch the Chaplain, Phramahasai, from the temple. Ten minutes later the official visitors arrived: Sripong Sawasri, the Governor of Nonthaburi; Gamol Porngul, the prison doctor; Cherdchai Wattanasil from Bangrak Police Station and the Execution Supervision Committee. At 3.30pm the registrar took the prisoners' fingerprints and the photographer took their photos. Prathom, the executioner, arrived 30 minutes later, along with the Chaplain. Prathom headed off to the execution room while Phramahasai stood silently, waiting for the Head of Custody, Rhienchai Vilaipid, to finishing reading aloud the execution order, which the three condemned then had to sign. The Chaplain began the 20 minute ritual at 4.20pm. The two men listened in silence with heads bowed, in acceptance of their fate. Ginggaew sat in front of them and was growing more and more distressed by the minute. She started to cry:

'I didn't do it. I didn't kill the boy. Please don't kill me, I didn't kill him.'

She fainted several times after that and had to be revived with smelling salts.

At 5pm Ginggaew was selected to be brought to the execution room first. The escorts helped her to her feet but she immediately crumpled to the ground. She sobbed that she felt too weak to stand, let alone walk. She continued to black out repeatedly while the escorts wondered what to do. Eventually it was decided to use a van to carry her the 800 metres from the office to the execution room. Her escorts managed to lift her on to the van. They drove her as far as the gazebo near the execution room and then stopped to give her some time to compose herself. She sat facing the roof of the temple. There was a table beside her with flowers, candles and incense. The escorts blindfolded her and placed the flowers in her hand—they would be used for the final asking of forgiveness. As she approached the room she had to be revived from another faint.

I found this very difficult to deal with. Between us we finally got the stricken woman to the cross. She cried while they bound her at the waist, shoulders, and elbows. Her arms were brought up over the beam in a position of prayer. Still, she struggled and tried vainly to break free. The escorts pulled across the screen and fixed it so that the white square indicated where her heart was. They then stepped away out of range. I walked to gun to load it and aim it at the target on the screen. I was aware that Ginggaew was still struggling. Normally once the prisoner was fixed to the cross they gave up fighting, but this was not the case with her. I secured the gun over her stifled sobs, locking it into position. When I was satisfied, I nodded at Prathom to take over. He took his position and at 5.40pm exactly he released ten bullets into Ginggaew's body.

Doctor Porngul went up to her and checked for the pulse and retina response. As expected, he confirmed her dead. The escorts quickly untied her body, which was bleeding profusely from the chest, and laid her face down on the floor. She jerked and twitched a little. This wasn't out of the ordinary but was distressing to witness. Her chest burst open and the blood looked like it would never stop flowing. They carried her into the morgue, the tiny room that we used just off the execution hall. I followed them just to make sure everything was alright. They placed her gently on the bed and we went out to prepare for the next one. What happened then will never leave me.

As the second prisoner, Gasem, was brought into the execution room, there was a sound from the morgue. I could see everything from where I was standing as the door was wide open—Ginggaew was trying to get up. The shocked escorts and I ran back to her. There was blood everywhere. One of the escorts rolled her over and pressed down on her back to accelerate the bleeding and help her die. Another escort, a real hard man, tried to strangle her to finish her off but I swept his arms away in disgust. We stood there watching her gasp for breath for I don't know how long, but it could only have been a minute or two. I was filled with pity for her. I couldn't help thinking that she was dying the way that little boy had died—except suffocating from blood instead of earth.

Meanwhile, Gasem had been shot. He died instantly from ten bullets. He had not resisted his death in any way, and spoke to nobody on the way to the cross. After the doctor confirmed that Gasem was definitely dead he checked on Ginggaew. Amazingly she was still breathing. It was a horrible, horrible situation. He told the escorts to put her back on the cross. The men complied, somewhat relieved to be able to just follow orders. It was a grim, nauseating job and they were covered in her blood when they turned to pull the screen across. This time the full quota of 15 bullets were used, and finally, she was dead.

You might wonder why we didn't just shoot her where she lay, but it would have been against the regulations. Also, I don't know that any of us could have stood so close to the young girl and pulled the trigger. As it was, the escorts moved as quickly as possible, each of us was concerned that her suffering should not be prolonged.

Pin had had to wait outside for ten minutes until Ginggaew was carried to the morgue for the second time. He was then brought in and tied to the cross. At 6.05pm Prathom pulled the trigger, sending 13 bullets into his back. The doctor went to check on him and discovered that he too was still alive, only just, but still breathing all the same. I loaded the gun again and Prathom shot a further ten bullets, this time killing him instantly. We were all in need of more than one stiff drink that evening.

In the bar that night my colleagues repeated what I had been thinking, that both Ginggaew and Pin had suffered like the child had suffered, with neither of them dying immediately. I couldn't begin to imagine the fear and pain that the little boy was subjected to. How a grown man can kill a six-year-old is just beyond me. By now I had three children of my own, and flashes of them when they were six and seven burnt into my head as I knocked back beer after beer. They were still babies at six years—babies who could walk and talk and who only expected people to treat them well. They hadn't learned to be suspicious yet.

Later in the newspapers the victim's mother spoke about Ginggaew. She said that she hired her to do the housework and mind her son. However, she found her to be lacking as a housekeeper—she spent too much time with the boy.

There are a couple of reasons why Ginggaew had such a terrible death. Firstly her heart wasn't on the left side as with most people. She most probably had Kartagener's Syndrome, which is when a person is born with their heart on the right-hand side instead of the left. And even if it was she wasn't secured firmly enough to the cross so she was able to move around, therefore the bullets would miss their target. It showed the importance of binding the prisoner as tightly as possible, for their own sake. I had my doubts when she was first pronounced dead. I thought I could detect some strain in her neck, and maybe that's why I followed the escorts to the morgue. The head should normally flop backwards with the cross being the only support for the limp body.

***

I am constantly asked about Ginggaew. She didn't think she deserved to die because she never physically harmed the child, not fully understanding that she was liable as an accomplice. She didn't get on with the couple; then they fired up and there was some discrepancy over her last wage packet. She wasn't highly educated and felt aggrieved over how she had been treated. She had minded their son for two months and formed a close attachment to him, and was perhaps even angry at being separated from him. So, unfortunately, she poured out her anger to her boyfriend who was an ex-con. She was also having an affair with Pin, who was married to Thongsuk, who received life imprisonment. He was a bad seed through and through. It was such a shame that Ginggaew ever got mixed up with him. His plot had led directly and indirectly to the deaths of four persons, including his own. At 28 he had a wife and a girlfriend—some women just like the dangerous types I suppose. If she had confided in a decent person she might have been merely encouraged to find a better job. Instead, her boyfriend came up with the kidnapping plan—which was to go completely awry beside the train tracks on that dark, awful night.

She was executed by a summary order, issued by Prime Minister Thanin. This meant that there was no opportunity to build up a defence and appeal for leniency in a court room. She was sentenced to death by the government and that was it. If you asked me whether I agreed with this I would have to say no. I think if it had had gone to court it would have resulted in her being sentenced to life imprisonment.

She didn't kill the boy; she became part of something that was completely out of her control and experience. She was guilty of kidnapping but a lawyer would have pointed out how she was badly kicked when she tried to protect the boy, and how she was treated by her employers in the first place. I suppose the government had to make an example of her, to warn any other domestics against this behaviour. We still have a few cases today of servants assaulting or killing their employers because they are being badly treated. At the end of the day you have to respect others. The case got widespread coverage because of the child, and the government probably felt they had to be seen to respond as efficiently as possible.

CHAPTER 10

By October 1984, the executioner Prathom Kreuapong had retired. I was going to miss my colleague. He had been an undertaker before working for Bang Kwang and was also into Black Magic, and loved to regale us with fantastic stories about his former career and hobby. Thinyo Janotarn was another executioner who was still active in the prison. Soon after Kreuapong left, Superintendent Sawat Sansern asked me to step into his office.

'Chavoret, could you be an executioner? I've already spoken to Chalore Nhumuang, the head of the execution team. He and Prathom warmly recommended you for the job. Will you do it?'

When I didn't reply he added, 'I wouldn't ask you if I didn't think you were up for the job. You would be second to Thinyo and it's not like there would be an execution every month. Just a few times a year.'

I'll be honest. I considered it an honour to be asked. The job required experience and skill. Plus I was being asked by the Superintendent himself. I knew I was a good worker. I wasn't corrupt and I didn't try to charm my superiors through licking ass or collecting college degrees. I just did my job to the best of my ability. It was obvious to me that I was liked and respected by the high-ranking officers. I had made a name for myself through my efficiency and my ability to act under pressure.

On a practical level the extra money could not be ignored. I was now the father of three children who I dearly wanted educated in the best schools I could afford. This would make a difference. I was still playing gigs to make ends meet, mostly weddings at the weekend. Tew was doing her bit too. The prison had hired her to sell food to the inmates' relatives; she ran a Somtam (papaya salad) stall. We were both working hard but not really gaining much from it. Every so often I would have to take out a loan to get us through a rough patch. The 2,000 baht per shooting would mean we could start saving money for the kids' future.

Once again I rose to the challenge and compliment.

'No problem sir. I will take it.'

I had played a vital role in the execution team for more than ten years now, first as escort and then as gun adjuster. I didn't differentiate much between the roles—that of actual executioner was no more part of the killing than gun adjuster or the one who held the flag. I have already described why I thought the escort had the worst job in the process. That look that the prisoner gives you, just as you stop outside his cell to collect him, pierces your very being. When I have trouble sleeping, it is that look of pure terror which appears in my mind's eye.

The escort is like the last friend in the world for the condemned. They get to hear the stories and tit-bits about the prisoner's life. One guy told me that he was being executed because his wife had failed to ask his lawyer to file a petition for him. Instead of encouraging the lawyer to pull out all the stops to save her husband's life, she slept with him. After chatting with the prisoner and maybe consoling him about his fate you then had to blindfold him and fasten him to a cross. That could seriously mess with your head.

I suppose that is why the team contained so many of us. Ten officers had ten duties surrounding the termination of one convict. No one could take the full brunt of the awful responsibility. I'll be honest again. I think it is a sin to take a man's life but I live in Thailand where we make people pay if they commit a dreadful crime. You murder someone—then you must lose your life too. An eye for an eye. It's not a perfect solution but there has to be an ultimate deterrent. I didn't take the job because I wanted to shoot people dead. If I had shown any signs of excitement or a thirst for blood I would never have been offered the position. A while ago there was one mean guy who really wanted to be an executioner. He used to chop the heads off cats and dogs, and revelled in the idea of killing criminals. He was never considered for the job, and later came to a bad end himself when he was burnt alive in a car crash.

There are some evil people out there, who are and always will be a danger to ordinary people. We arrest them for murder, and perhaps they show remorse, or perhaps they don't. But what's the point of feeding them in jail for the rest of their lives? What good is that to anyone? Social services people would advise that a person becomes a criminal because of their upbringing or peers. They are influenced or manipulated into carrying out their evil acts. The criminology guys advise that there are born criminals—they are lacking, or have too much of, some chemical in the brain. I say that criminals, no matter how they evolved, should be punished according to the crime they have committed. There was a case here recently in Thailand: A young boy at military school was beaten within an inch of his life by a gang, and was left permanently injured. The boys who did this to him were charged with physical assault and received sentences of two and three years. Meanwhile, the victim's parents have just about lost their son; he will never be who he was before the beating. This is hardly reflected in those flimsy sentences. An eye for an eye would surely bring more justice to that family.

***

On 10 October 1984 the Superintendent sent a letter to the Department of Correction asking for permission to grant two appointments; Thinyo would be 1st Executioner and Chavoret Jaruboon would be 2nd Executioner.

He received an official reply on 4 December.

'The DOC has considered your application. Execution is ordered by the court and is the duty of a prison to carry out. Therefore, the Superintendent of Bang Kwang is entitled to assign any officer he wishes to enable the smooth operation of execution, without the express approval of the DOC. The position of Executioner is treated as any other position. With that in mind the DOC is not required to issue an official appointment. If the Superintendent of Bang Kwang requires two executioners then he should go ahead and appoint them himself.'

And so began the next 20 years of my life.

***

My first killings, in my new position within the execution team, were of a gang who had shot a market trader after they tried to rob him, and had then panicked and shot two young policemen, killing one.

The crime had happened on 23 November 1980, at Saphan 2, the fresh food market on Lardprao Road in the Banggapi District of Bangkok.

38-year-old Lhiam Kiat-opas was working at his fish stall as usual. A blue Datsun pulled up at the market place and three men got out. They walked straight up to Lhiam. One of the men reached out and tore a necklace from the neck of the fish vendor. The chain was made of pure gold and contained three tiny Buddha figures; it was worth approximately 50,000 baht. Lhiam was a brave man and fought back. However, he was no match for the .45 pistol that was suddenly produced. He was shot at point blank rage and died instantly. There was panic in the market with people screaming and running for cover. The three men walked back to their car as if they were out for a stroll, ignoring the chaos around them.

Meanwhile, two young police officers were driving by the market and saw all the commotion. Before they could respond, the windows of the Datsun were lowered and the robbers opened fire. A 21-year-old officer called Anek Anantachaigul died after being shot through the back of his helmet. His partner, 23-year-old Surapong Boonchai, was shot through his forehead and right leg. When the killers left, the wounded officer was carried to the hospital by the market people.

The following day a Mr Yuttapol Pummalee returned his rented Datsun to Klongtoey Car Rentals. During the customary inspection a blood stain was discovered inside the car. Details of the previous day's shooting spree had been all over the evening news. The suspicious employee rang the police and was able to detain his client until they arrived. The officers told the 26-year-old that he would have to accompany them back to the police station as they needed to ask him about the stain. They put him in the back of their vehicle and drove off. The lights turned red at Dusit Thani Junction and Yuttapol seized the opportunity to jump out of the car and start running. He was caught minutes later and asked by the police why he was trying to escape—after all they just wanted to ask him some questions about a blood stain.

Yuttapol must have felt the gig was up because he folded immediately:

'Yesterday, my friends and I robbed a fish merchant at the Saphan 2 market.'

He went on to tell the officers where his friends, Narong Pingaew, Lhee Daengaram and Samran Pingaew were hiding. They were still in Bangkok, staying in Wat Koh Suwannaram. There, on 13 December, the police arrested 25-year-old Narong and 38-year-old Lhee and then a little later that day they arrested Samran in the province of Suraburi. The men were charged with the robbery and murder of Lhiam Kiat-opas, and the murder of Officer Anek Anantachaigul.

The case went to court. Thanks to Yuttapol's confession, and plenty of witnesses from the market place, the four men were found guilty as charged. They were handed the death penalty in view of the severe nature of the crime and the fact that it happened in a public place, thus endangering the public at large. The four men were also ordered to pay a fine of 50,000 baht to the victims' families.

On 23 November 1984, fours years to the day after committing the two murders in the market place, 3 of the 4 killers of Lhiam Kiat-opas were to meet their just reward, and I would take my place alongside Thinyo in the execution room—my first time behind the gun. I don't recall what happened to Yuttapal, the first man to confess. His fate was none of my business.

I was informed that morning that there would be an execution later in the evening. I was allowed to finish my shift early and drove home to take a nap and change my uniform. I wanted to be sure that I was completely refreshed and at ease. The day before, the family and I had celebrated my 36th birthday. I had gone to the temple to make a merit, as I always do on my birthday. This is a Thai or Buddhist practice which might seem funny to outsiders. I made an offering of a Sungkatan basket. This is a plastic yellow basket filled with essentials for the monks: toothpaste, umbrella, tea, sandals, soap, and a robe. You offer it to the monk out of kindness and a longing to help maintain the Buddhist system. The items have to be bought new and specifically for the monk. You can also make a merit by buying the life of an animal, obviously the bigger and more expensive, the better. If a cow is going to be butchered you can offer ample money to save its life. If you couldn't stretch to a cow, you might be able to buy a cage of birds, or turtles, and set them free. So you do your good act and silently ask for something in return. You do good to have good happen to you. Therefore, if you do bad…

***

I had personally checked my gun at 9am, believing that I would never truly trust anyone else to do it. I wasn't too nervous; I had so much experience by now in these matters. I slept, showered, quickly dressed, and was back at the prison with plenty of time to spare.

At 5pm the escorts brought in Narong and Samran. Narong was tied to the cross on the right and Samran was tied on the cross to the left. They were to die together, Narong by Thinyo's hand and Samran by mine. At 5.07pm the red flag was lowered. I fired ten shots into Samran, and Thinyo fired eight into Narong. The doctor came through and confirmed the two men to be dead. They were untied by the escorts and carried into the morgue. I busied myself with emptying and reloading the gun. We had about 15 minutes to go before the third convict arrived. I glanced at Thinyo and he looked like he wanted to ask something but thought better of it. I decided to make it easier for him.

'Well brother, what about the third guy?'

He relaxed his features and suggested I do it. In fact he asked me to. It really wasn't a big deal. I didn't have to talk to these men in their last moments. I didn't hand them a pen and paper and help them with their spellings in the letters to their families. I didn't know if they were scared or not, or whether they were obediently listening to the Chaplain or scowling in resistance at his teachings. All I had to do was pull a trigger at a target on a screen—it is very easy to empty your mind and just shoot. Especially when it is your job and you are being closely watched by your superiors and government officials.

At 5.20pm Lhee quietly followed his escorts into the room. At 5.24pm I saluted him through the screen and leant over the gun. The flag lowered and I pulled the trigger, but nothing happened. Red-faced I realised I had forgotten to unlock the gun. I felt a jolt of surprise from the viewing box, where the officials stood. I didn't dare look up to meet anyone's eyes. Instead, I kept focused on the gun. Another second and I had unlocked it and put 11 bullets through the screen, killing Lhee instantly.

It hit me later in the evening. I thought about my kids being asked by their friends, or their friends' parents about what their father did. I imagined some of the kids in their class proudly announcing that their father was a dentist, a soldier, a businessman or whatever. Then my child might suddenly realise that they weren't delighted to inform teacher that dad was the executioner in Bang Kwang prison. I worried about nobody ever being brave enough to date my daughter, after hearing what her old man did for a living. I fretted that first night that I had ruined her chances for a husband and family of her own.

On the other hand, because I was the executioner I had to remain in Bang Kwang. Prison officers were always living under the threat of being moved to another prison. This way I could never be moved away from my family, or alternatively spend long precious hours commuting to work. At the end of the day I felt that I played an important role in the country's justice system. My boss needed me, since nobody else wanted to do this job. And he was right about infrequent executions; in 70 or 80 years of the death sentence, there have only been 300 people killed in this way. Previously the condemned was flogged 90 times and then tied to a small cross in the ground, which meant the prisoner was seated with his back to it and his arms outstretched, and beheaded. Three executioners were always standing by to make sure the job was done.

Christians always ask about the relevance of the cross, whether it means something particular, but there is no hidden meaning about its role in an execution. It has nothing to do with Jesus Christ being crucified by the Romans or about His resurrection. It is simply the best shape for the job. A man's arms can be spread out across it and it is the perfect shape for taking someone's limp weight after they have been shot, as in the case of the bigger cross. If the condemned was a member of the Royal Family or a high-ranking officer then a better class of execution was required—they would be beaten to death with a sweet-smelling stick.

There were plenty of rituals involved in those days, including dousing with holy water, meditating and praying aloud to the gods at a nearby shrine. Then, in 1934, King Rama VII abolished beheading, deciding that shooting was more humane for both criminal and executioner. I must say that I could not have chopped off someone's head with a sword—there is no way on earth I would have been able to do that. It was horrific. Three men would be involved in the beheading. One would try to distract the condemned man by stomping around, making noise, while another would make the deadly strike. A third man would stand to the side, just in case. All three were considered part of the ritual. There are some incredible black and white photographs of an actual beheading on display at the museum in the Department of Correction, in the Phranakorn district of Bangkok. Just make sure you don't visit the museum right after eating—some of the stuff on display could prove a bit traumatic for your stomach.

***

I was always conscious of looking after my sanity. I was not naïve—I knew that plenty of prison staff who had been involved with the executions didn't die in a hospital bed. Prathom, whose place I had taken as executioner, had formerly been an undertaker so he was used to dealing with death. I had led a more sheltered life, playing the guitar, and even my stint in the army was not ample preparation for what I as doing. Depression and addiction were part of the set-up. To counter this I took up chanting, and went to a monk for some guidance. I read up about it and taught myself how to do it effectively. Chanting is great for aiding concentration and helping my confidence.

Originally I had applied to do a proper course in Sukothai Thammathirat and Ramkhamhaeng open universities, but I just couldn't afford it. Albeit, I probably could have scraped the money together but if I had, my daughter would have missed out on attending university, and my kids are everything to me. My father had taught me that you must do the best that you can as a parent. He showed me how with his consistent generosity to me and my brother.

CHAPTER 11

Foreign prisoners complain a lot! I realise that we should try and understand their different cultures and customs. It is bad enough to be jailed but it must be really harsh to be held in a foreign prison, far from home. Nevertheless you would not believe the time wasted on sorting out silly complaints from serious ones. Black prisoners accuse us of racism and everyone else complains about living in cramped, unhealthy conditions. But Bang Kwang is a prison, not a hotel.

One Indian prisoner lodged a complaint that he never received the 30,000 baht that he claimed was posted to him. There was an investigation and the DOC had to question us over our security measures. I mean, who puts all that money in an envelope and shoves it in the post nowadays? Of course we prison guards do try to understand the inmates' problems. It would be foolish to ignore genuine complaints or else we might end up with another riot on our hands.

The farang prisoners are, on the whole, treated quite well by the staff and Thai prisoners. Generally Thai people really look up to farangs and their western ways. Farangs find it very easy to hire Thais to do their errands, inside and outside of Bang Kwang. Most of the foreign inmates are here because of drug trafficking. Some are small-time criminals while others are or were members of huge criminal groups making millions of baht from drugs.

The foreigners are distributed over all the wings. If we locked them all in together and there was a dispute we might have a difficulty interpreting them. Therefore, each wing is usually made up of 99% Thai and the rest foreign. Because of the different treatment meted out to foreigners, resentment can build up. For instance, Thai convicts are only allowed family visits at a certain time, even if their relatives have travelled all the way from the outskirts of Thailand for a surprise visit. Meanwhile an embassy will contact us and tell us that 'Mom' got on a plane and flew all the way over to see her son, so what are we to do? We have to make an allowance and let her see him.

And now, of course, it is nearly a fashionable or touristy thing to do. All these young people, full of ideals, who turn up to visit the foreign prisoners after watching *Green Mile* or *Dead Man Walking* and we have to cater for them. I think there are far too many of them but I suppose they don't cause any trouble. They tend to stick out because they look more frightened than the inmates on death row, although I appreciate that it is quite an intimidating experience for young farangs who have never been near a prison before. When you visit you have to be prepared—dress modestly and remember to be polite to the prison staff. You will have to shout to be heard as you will be separated from the guy you are visiting by a few feet, and also you and your prisoner will be only two of a large group of noisy relatives and loved ones. You can bring gifts of food and books, but just in case you are thinking about it, stuff like nude photos will probably be taken off you!

Some years ago families of foreign prisoners who couldn't afford to visit Thailand as much as they wished got the brilliant idea of putting up notices in guest house and hotels with information of their loved ones, in the hope that some of the many tourists might visit them. I completely understand their anxiety. I don't know what I would do if one of my children was jailed in another country.

There are two other groups to contend with, in relation to the foreign prisoners. The first are the ones who are appointed by the embassies. They might be the wives of officials who have volunteered to visit and meet the prisoners, and they are very reasonable and do not cause us any trouble. Then there are the 'missionary' groups. Some of the prisoners are converted to Christianity and find themselves with an extra tube of toothpaste for Christmas. When I was in charge of Ward 1 the missionary groups used to throw a Christmas party for the foreign prisoners. There would be 30 to 40 inmates who were allowed to go to the party which was held in the wing. Food and drink would be brought in specially and it was an enjoyable few hours, especially for me, since I could speak English.

The different groups furnish us with a list of whom they want to visit, but I think they also have a hidden agenda. I believe they visit everyone on the list to find out who has money. The one with money receives a lot more visits than the one without. Bear in mind that the ones with the money are usually big-time drug lords and now they have this group hard at work for them, emailing their every complaint to all and sundry. I sometimes even find myself suspicious about the inmates' letters to these groups. Are they full of codes and actually trying to use these people to keep in touch with people on the outside about supplying drugs?

Then there is the problem with diet. The farangs complained that the food we served was too spicy for them. So we cooked white rice separately for them in small plastic bags. Then they complained that they weren't getting enough food. So we allowed them to see how we prepare the meals from the quantities that we had in the kitchen and they rewarded us by stealing food. Then they said that they weren't receiving equal amounts of food. So we began to measure it all out.

Right now we have 500 foreign convicts from 45 different countries and things can get quite complicated. The white prisoners will eat the white rice. The Asians normally don't touch the white rice, except if they are from Hong Kong and hold British passports. Then people from Taiwan and Taipei get upset because they want to have a choice of rice and feel they are losing out otherwise. Then the Japanese embassy told us that they were just as civilized as America so why weren't all their people just offered the white rice? Before you know it we almost had an international rice crisis on our hands. Although, everyone seems to get on with the Thai prisoners, which is nice.

Anyway, it gives the foreigners something to do. They love lodging complaints—sending five copies of one document to their embassies and any other organisation that might help them. The embassies are kept very busy by their own criminals and sometimes they are conned by their own legal system. I personally welcome their inspections. It keeps us on our toes and forces us to keep changing. The embassies never support what a prisoner has done; they just need to know that he is being treated properly. They double check everything we do in Bang Kwang and we must be able to answer any question put to us. The prison staff don't like when there is a complaint about us so we try to ensure that we do our jobs well.

We once had a German who was on parole. He was a child molester. The embassy didn't approve of him being out on parole but one of their volunteers was compelled to sign the papers. He agreed to stay in a church in Bangkok and not leave the country. However, when we tried to contact him two days later he had gone. It transpired the German embassy had to issue a temporary visa for anyone with a German passport. Because of that we cancelled parole as an option. The normal procedure now is for them to spend eight years here in Bang Kwang and then they are sent back home. It is more beneficial to us to return them to their own country. No good can come out of keeping them here, taking up valuable space. I think that a prison sentence of more than ten years would be too much for the average man. A Hong Kong prisoner wrote to us that he was on parole in England and living with his family. Then we heard that when the English authorities sent him home he was jailed in his own country. Not all crimes lead to long sentences but the penalty for dealing in drugs in Thailand is severe.

As to the organisations that campaign against the death penalty, I would love them to take in two or three hardened criminals and then see how they feel. 69 countries have the death penalty today so there must be some sort of necessity for it. I remember once when an Australian businessman was shot in Thailand, his supporters did not want to know about his killers— what was their background and how they did become killers—they just wanted to know when I was going to shoot them. The same attitude prevails when a white girl is raped; nobody cares why, they just want the rapist punished.

***

I cannot emphasise enough to the people who come to see Thailand—be very careful! Be on your guard. If you come here to sell or buy drugs there are plenty of people waiting to catch you, including police who will falsify evidence to arrest you. Drugs are completely illegal here. There are spies everywhere, especially watching for foreigners who might break our laws. The prostitute that you sleep with just might be working for the police. Thailand is more dangerous than you think. It is quite easy to get yourself arrested if you don't know any better. Do you know that if you are driving a vehicle that accidentally knocks someone down and injures them, you could find yourself charged with attempted murder? If that happens you better have plenty of money to 'help' the police keep you out of jail.

Unfortunately, the number of foreign prisoners had increased over the years. Thailand attracts lots of people who think they can make their fortune here. Unemployment is rife. The Russians gangs in Pattaya kidnap Thai women and send them abroad to their brothels. Foreign criminals, I can't remember the nationality, tricked a compatriot to come to Thailand and open up a bar. When he did so, they killed him and stole all his money. Poor Africans, from Nigeria and Ghana in particular, end up carrying drugs and then end up here as a result. The death penalty is not a solution but it should function as a strong deterrent. However, with the increasing number of foreigners being arrested and convicted here, I am not so sure that it does.

CHAPTER 12

Being a prison guard is a tough job and not for the fainthearted. Yet no matter how tough the staff at Bang Kwang, or any prison on the planet for that matter, the merest hint of the word 'riot' will probably shake their collective confidence, however temporarily. It was in 1985 that we had what you might call the mother of all riots and it couldn't have happened at a worse time for the already stretched and busy staff. Anyone who has ever worked in a prison will tell you that a riot is a constant threat; they are part and parcel of the whole experience. The best that you can hope for is that it doesn't spread to involve the entire population of convicts.

About 20 years ago Tawee Choosap was the Director-General of DOC. He felt very passionately about his job and about his role in the prison system. It irritated him to know that society in general held no curiosity about the prisons or prison life and what knowledge they did have was probably very clichéd or stereotypical. He wished to change all that. He established a sort of Open Day for prisons, which the media and public were invited to. It went down very well and resulted in the 'Visiting Day'.

'Visiting Day' was a very special occasion for the inmates because it was the only time in the year that they could welcome their families without bars between them. This only applied to those who had a good grade. You remember how I said that each prisoner was graded from very bad, bad, satisfactory, good, and very good to excellent depending on his behaviour? Well, first offenders were usually given an immediate grade of 'satisfactory' on their arrival while a convict who was on his second prison sentence in five years received the 'bad' grade. After that it was up to the individual to get himself promoted or demoted by the guards. I suppose you could compare it to school but at least this helped the staff to identify potential trouble and also motivate the prisoner to obtaining a better grade if he was to be put forward for a royal pardon. The pardon doesn't mean that he is immediately unleashed on the outside world again; it just mean a reduction in his prison sentence.

On Visiting Day the well-behaved criminal could receive up to ten relatives who would usually bring a picnic with them. In fact it was much more than one day. The event lasted ten days each time—twice a year. Therefore, for 20 days out of the year the prisoner could hug his wife, children, parents and siblings. He could even have a proper discussion with his lawyer. The only thing he could not do was have sex with his spouse or girlfriend. There just wasn't the room. Usually a prisoner's family could only visit one day a week, Friday, when they could peer at their loved one through the prison bars. The celebration was usually held near Mothers' And Fathers' Day, which was the birthdays of Her Majesty Queen's Siritkit and His Majesty King Bhumiphol, on 12 August and 5 December. So reducing prisoners' sentences was a royal version of making merit; they helped out the most miserable class in society and would be rewarded for it in this life or the next.

To accommodate and cater for the extra thousands of visitors, the staff at Bang Kwang had to work very hard indeed. The football pitch and the auditorium, which were both to the right of the prison's entrance, were the specified 'visiting' location—or, if you like, the reception area. The auditorium is probably our biggest enclosed space and has a stage. The prison also rents huge tents, and hundreds of tables and chairs. It also involved a huge amount of administration. The family contacted the prison and made a request to visit. They would have to furnish us with identification for each relative, along with their census records.

I was usually stationed at the security tower between the six wings and the football field and was in charge of security. It always meant long hard days for the prison guards because we were constantly short of staff, in relation to the numbers of visitors and prisoners. Therefore, if you got a break you were lucky. My day would normally begin about 7am when I would do a complete check of the football ground and auditorium. At 7.30am the excited prisoners who were receiving visitors would be escorted to the auditorium where they eagerly lined up to be frisked. Their relatives would not arrive until 8.30am and it was a busy hour and a half to make sure that everything was as it should be. The relatives had to pass through a sort of metal detector and I would also frisk them. It was quite a big operation, though the mood was always light. Administration would already have sent them a letter informing them what they could or could not bring. The relatives could stay until 11.30am and they would have to leave until the afternoon session. This meant that the prisoners had to be frisked four times, before and after meeting their families. Back-breaking work for the prison guard! All the normal day-to-day running of the prison had to continue so we were literally cramming extra tasks into each day.

It was an enjoyable time for everyone involved. During those two sets of ten days Bang Kwang was a warmer place, where everyone was smiling, hugging, kissing. There was a real sense of compassion in the air and the staff were always very moved by it. It was customary to see the younger prisoners fall asleep with their heads in their mothers' laps. Prisoners might introduce a favourite prison guard to his family, who would fall over themselves to be welcoming.

It is also a very productive time, commercially speaking. There were lots of stands selling food and items made by the prisoners themselves, which were usually run by relatives of the guards. Tew, my good wife, ran a food stand during Visiting Day and made a whopping 10,000 baht in sales every day. She and her sister would get up at 4am to prepare the food and I would usually find myself being roped in to fetch the ingredients. The visitors wanted to shower the prisoners with food and anything else they could lay their hands on. You can surely imagine it, especially if you are a parent—you would spend freely to ease your own mind that you were doing all that you could for your unfortunate child.

***

4 August 1985 was the last day of the first 'visiting season' of the year. There were a lot of people as usual, fanned out across the football pitch, sitting in their family groups and enjoying the good weather and each other. The scene was more suited to a beach than a tough prison. I was on my ninth day of frisking the prisoners and visitors from my check-point at the front gate of the security tower. It was 10am and everything was running smoothly, except for my aching body. I stretched my back and tried to improve my stance so that I didn't slouch. I had been working straight for the nine days and was verging on exhaustion. As you can imagine the prison staff had to be extra vigilant during this time. The guards want to appear more flexible and friendly but of course you wonder if one of the smiling families is going to try their hand at a rescue mission.

And then there are the prisoners themselves. They might take the opportunity to act out some frustration, although I tend to believe that the prisoners would keep each other in line because they are in the company of their loved ones. Each convict would protect his own family from harm, and if a guy was fool enough to capture another's daughter or sister then he would be leaving his own womenfolk open to attack.

I had been working incessantly for the past hour and was ravenous. It was approaching the end of the morning shift when the visitors would be asked to leave. We would then make our rounds to ensure everything was ok and all the prisoners were accounted for. The visitors would return at approximately 1pm for the afternoon shift which would finish about 3pm. Once the visitors were gone I planned to have a good meal before getting ready for the afternoon. Just as I was mulling over what I would like to eat, one of my assistants raced over to me looking tremendously excited over something. In between gasps of hot air he managed to tell me, 'Sir, something is happening in Wing 6!'

I felt a cold shiver in the pit of my empty stomach and asked him to be more specific.

'I'm not 100 % sure but it kinda looks like a riot.'

This was bad—really, really bad. In less than an hour hundreds of happy relatives would start walking from the football field towards the entrance. To do this they would have to pass by the front gate of Wing 6 where they would have to stop and wait in order to be frisked before they could leave the prison's premises. In other words they would make an easy and large target for angry criminals who couldn't meet with their families because of their low grade. It might sound overly dramatic to say that, as I stood there with my breathless assistant, I quickly envisioned a blood bath of impressive proportions, but you have to remember the context. This wasn't some boarding school; this was Bang Kwang.

I raced over to the gate at Wing 6 hoping against hope that he was wrong. Maybe it was just the usual run-of-the-mill gang fight. These happened frequently and only involved key players. They could be bloody but relatively short. It was a two minute run to the gate from the tower. I gripped the bars of the gate. There was a security guard stationed here 24 hours a day. You just didn't want to think of the consequences of the emptying out of the inhabitants of Wing 6 on to the unprepared streets. Beyond the bars, the inner gate is a big solid metal door with a huge lock on it. There is also a slot which can be uncovered to peek inside to check on things, like you would see on the door of a police station's cell. We would use it when a prisoner was preparing to be brought to court. You would have to check that the right prisoner was standing there waiting, without weapons or accomplices. Of course we also used it regularly during the visiting season, to ensure that the right prisoner was waiting to join the right family.

The officer at the outer gate was obviously hoping for assistance or direction. He beckoned me immediately and whispered:

'Sir, they have taken Officers Gamol and Prasit as hostages.'

Shit, shit, shit. I asked him what exactly was going on.

'I don't know the details Sir but they are mounting a riot for sure'.

I babbled at him, 'We are going to be in big trouble. There are over 1,000 inmates and family outside who will be shortly heading this way. We have an hour and that's all!'

I took a deep breath; there was no point in panicking him any more than he was. I had to pull myself together. I told the officer to lock the inner and outer gate of

Wing 6 and not to open them, under any circumstances, until he received instructions from our superiors. He locked the gates without a word. We both knew that we were locking some of our colleagues in with the madness but this is what we had been trained to do in these circumstances.

I climbed up the wall to get a view of what was going on in Wing 6. It was like a scene from a Hollywood movie—all that was needed was a Johnny Cash or Elvis soundtrack. The inmates were in groups spread over the wing. Some were wearing bandanas which might have made me smile in a different setting. They all appeared to be armed, some with blocks of wood and some with metal poles with pointed ends that looked to me like medieval lances. They must have taken the poles from the equipment room and sharpened them in the workshop. A few of the men looked high and it was later discovered that they had stolen and consumed paint thinning substance, also from the workshop. I couldn't see any officers; there are usually ten to every wing—ten for every 1,000 prisoners. You do the math! On Visiting Day two officers from each wing had to accompany his prisoners to the football field, leaving behind eight men to supervise a fractious village of convicts.

Within minutes, Prathin Glaisung, Chief of the Custody Section, reported the riot to the Superintendent, who immediately ordered the outer and inner gates of the rest of the wings, 1 to 5, to be locked until further notice. Then an announcement was made over the loud speakers informing everyone that a riot was taking place. The visitors were asked to remain calm and make their way to the auditorium to await instructions. The convicts—the 'visitees'— were asked to line up at the end of the football pitch. Meanwhile the people running the stalls had started to swiftly pack up their belongings. I had a quick look to make sure that Tew was one of them. We would have a terrible row later when she returned with our three children to watch the chaos, along with the rest of Nonthaburi. We lived in a house that was provided by the government, down the road from the prison.

I couldn't believe it when I spied my family calmly taking in the proceedings. I charged out and told Tew to take the children away to some place safe. And what did she do? She waited until I left and then turned to our eldest and told him to take his younger brother and sister over to his Uncle Oud's dormitory at Klong Prem so that she could remain to watch the rest of the show. It has become a family joke now but I was still mad at her days later.

With as many staff as we could spare, we led the nervous relatives towards the exit point at the security tower; women and children were first in line, followed by the men. As I had foreseen, the crowd were subject to taunts and insults. We all just gritted our teeth and grimly prepared to ignore it. But we couldn't ignore the missiles. Bottles, plates and stones were hurled at the crowd, which understandably panicked and started to run towards the main road. Women tried to huddle shocked and screaming children to themselves to protect them. Thankfully no one was hurt. I was also grateful for the fact that the visitees didn't try to take advantage of the panic and follow their loved ones to the outside world, or didn't quickly form an army to take on Wing 6 and punish them for the maltreatment of their families. It could easily have gone either way. While I was busy at the front gate, a couple of officers were retrieving weapons from the armoury in the security tower and the administrative officers were ringing around the various police stations for assistance.

When the last family member had been sent safely through the gate we were ordered to lead the waiting prisoners from the football field to where we kept those in solitary confinement. They would have to wait there until we got the situation under control, for their own safety. A few minutes later dozens of police officers arrived from Nonthaburi police station. Sawas Sansern, our Superintendent, had rang the Director General of DOC for assistance. He responded by ordering the police and prison officers to spread out, covering as much of Bang Kwang as possible. Some senior officers attempted to identify and talk to the ring leaders of the riot and open some sort of negotiations. There were dozens of ring leaders, which didn't help matters. They ordered their comrades-in-arms to gather all the tables and chairs from the canteen and stack them behind the inner gate to support it in case of an attack. They also had hostages—two guards.

Our officers kept asking the men to remain calm, and eventually this led to the hostages, Officers Gamol Sukpan and Prasit Taptimsri, being safely released. I don't really think that the two men were ever in real danger. They were unpopular as prison guards and were probably held briefly for a laugh more than anything else. However, if we thought this signalled an end to the trouble we were sadly mistaken. Things started to kick off again around mid-day. It turned out that the prisoners whose behaviour prohibited them from having visitors had been very busy otherwise—making booze from fermented fruit. So we had hardened criminals running wild, angry, frustrated, some high and now most of them drunk. They decided that they should look for some new recruits and started to throw things across the wall into Wing 5, by way of invitation to join their revolution. Fuelled by fruit the inmates at 6 began to roar, clap, stamp their feet and hammer at the bars. They formed a pyramid using the tables, thus making it easier for the men at 5 to join them.

Meanwhile, it was lunch-time. It was decided that we should feed the inmates regardless of the situation. We could have tried to starve them in order to break their hold, but then any 6 prisoners who were not party to the revolt might join their mates out of hunger and anger. I suppose we also hoped that the food might soak up the alcohol. Since we couldn't enter the wing I had to push the food cart just past the inner gate of 6 and then stop. I slid open the peak hole and was told politely by the prisoner sent to accept the food.

'Thank you Sir. I'll handle it from here.'

I nodded stiffly in acquiescence. We both pretended that I had a choice.

The Superintendent was trying to negotiate with them. He kept asking the inmates to choose one representative he could speak with, but they just refused point-blank. They told him that they would only speak with the Minister of Interior, General Sithi Jirarod. Nevertheless, he did discover what the riot was all about. A politician's promise was causing all this trouble—a promise that could never be kept. Someone had publicly promised all prisoners that he would personally make a proposal to the Minister of Interior to submit a petition for a Royal Pardon on the occasion of the funeral of Her Majesty Rampaipannee. She was the wife of His Majesty Rama VII. His rashness acted like a burning cigarette on oil—it blew the place up. Amnesty was every prisoner's dream and fantasy, and no politician could casually promise them one. The Royal Family usually granted the Royal Pardon to prisoners on special occasions; special *happy* occasions, which a funeral was most definitely not. Inevitably, the convicts were bitterly disappointed when no pardon proved forthcoming, and naturally the politician denied promising anything later.

To be honest the inmates were being a bit unrealistic with their expectations. The whole process of granting amnesty takes a long time to complete. The Minister of Interior can only submit a proposal to the Royal Family or their representatives, for a mass amnesty. He certainly cannot rush the Family into making a decision. The prisoners on death row have up to 60 days after receiving their sentence to petition for their own amnesty. But then they could be left waiting for 12 months before they hear anything back.

***

The situation was worsening all the time. One wall separates each wing from the other. Prisoners at 5 who had been enticed to join now issued a similar invite to those in 4. The chaos was contagious, spreading quickly from wing to wing. Inmates broke into the offices and factories and started to systematically destroy all around them. They helped themselves to anything that could be used as, or fashioned into, a weapon. The Superintendent asked for the megaphone and begged the prisoners in 6 to calm down and return to their cells. Oddly, they promised to take it down a notch but were completely against returning to their own quarters. He issued the same request to the prisoners in 4 and 5. They issued the same response as 6.

Over 100 more police officers arrived at the prison. They spread out to prevent any escapes, and try to limit the protest to Wing 6. Shortly after their arrival they were joined by a group of Commandos. Police General Suwan Rattanashuen from the Department of Special Affairs turned up with Sanid Rujinarong, the Director General of DOC and other senior officers from the Ministry of Interior. At 12.30pm a meeting was called. Our Superintendent described the whole situation in detail and they studied an aerial map of Bang Kwang. Their meeting was disrupted 30 minutes later when the convicts resumed throwing things over the wall and chanting, 'We won't work, we'll just fucking eat!'

At 1.10pm the men elected a representative who was demanding to speak to prominent politicians, members of the National Assembly and, last but not least, the media. He wished to issue the prisoners' demands at 2pm. The prisoners had also furnished themselves with banners which they held proudly aloft for all to see. The messages varied little—'We would rather die if we don't get amnesty,' and, 'We were promised amnesty.'

At 1.30pm the police and prison officers removed all fuel from the prison wings to prevent anyone from thinking how wonderful it would be to set the prison on fire. The Superintendent told the administrative officers to digs out the files of all the ring leaders and study their profiles. Knowledge is power. One of the officer hostages, Gamol, was brought before the Superintendent to describe in detail what had happened from the very beginning.

'Prasit and I were on duty in Wing 6. The first sign of trouble was when the prisoner Munggorn (Dragon) approached us. He was carrying a metal bar that had been sharpened to a point at one end, which he shoved at my neck as he told us: "You officers must get out of this wing now because we are about to have a revolution." We had no choice but to leave. The other leaders are Vipop Phrahanthongchai and Noi Chaimard.'

The two were well known to all the prison guard through their constant complaints. Every month, without fail, they submitted two to three complaints about living conditions in the jail.

Gamol continued: 'Noi led dozens of inmates to take over the canteen. He climbed up on to a table and gave a speech to rouse the men to action. He was working the men up into a rage against the prison staff. When they appeared excited enough he instructed them to spread themselves throughout Wing 6 but to be careful to always stay in groups. He continued seducing the men with his wrath and it wasn't long before he was joined in the canteen by over 1,000 inmates, who started to shout, "No amnesty? We would rather die.'"

Noi Chaimard was a hardened criminal at 40 years of age. He was an extremely intelligent and articulate man, which made him more dangerous in our eyes. He had been imprisoned here before after being charged with murder. Now he had returned after being arrested and charged for attempted murder. Dragon was 26, and was in prison for a kidnapping and murder in the Lopburi Province. I don't think any of the officers were surprised at their instigating this riot; they were born troublemakers through and through and were a constant thorn in our sides.

The staff was made aware that there were worried families waiting outside the jail, wondering if they were going to be let in to resume their visit with their relative. They would have also been anxious about the welfare of their relative if the riot escalated. The prison made an announcement that Visiting Day and normal visitation hours were temporarily cancelled due to the ongoing disorder. They would have to wait until the following day to hear if normal visiting hours had been established. The prison also took the time to reassure the families that the law abiding convicts would be protected at all costs. However we would be reacting strongly to anyone who was taking part in the riot.

Meanwhile the rabble-rousing continued. There was a tough group of prisoners who called themselves 'Samurai', but they were nothing like their namesakes. They lacked the grace and dignity of the Samurais and were in reality a bunch of gangsters who liked to pick on the weaker inmates. They were the biggest contributors to the riot. They were the ones who convinced the inmates who wanted to return to their cells that if they did so they would just be beaten up by the prison guards. So it was to their own good to stay rioting with them. Some of the foreign prisoners had also been enticed to join in. We could hear the riot leaders urging their forces to fight until they dropped because it would be worth it if they were able to obtain amnesty. They kept demanding that the alleged promise of amnesty be kept. They started to organise their campaign in a more efficient manner and got themselves lawyers. These lawyers, inmates who had a background in law, from Wings 4 and 5, went to the canteen to submit their support for Wing 6 and offer their expertise. They gave a couple of encouraging speeches and then set about writing up the prisoners' proposals for negotiations.

At 1.40 in the afternoon the inmates were told by one of the leaders to start conserving water. They were obviously planning a long campaign. The small prison shop was overrun and its products; cartons of milk, soft drinks, tinned fruit and vegetables and cigarettes, were seized and dispensed to the rioters free of charge. We could hear the men cheering and clapping in their appreciation of the free bounty. A megaphone was taken from an office in Wing 6 and became the means for communicating with the outside world.

At 1.50pm one of the ring leaders addressed the journalists and camera crews standing at the gates of the prison. The prisoner asked the media to help aid the inmates in their appeal for amnesty. They hoped that the media would put pressure on Sanya Thammasak, President of the Privy Council, to give the inmates what they wanted.

At 2pm the Director-General of DOC appointed the Vice Director-General, Vijid Thongkum, to resolve the situation. The guy with the megaphone continued to address the journalists. The riot would not stop until the prisoners' demands were met. They realised that their actions were wrong and they were sorry that they had been driven to these lengths. All they wished was to be allowed a second chance to return to society and show themselves to be good citizens. They wanted to make their contribution towards making Thailand a great place to live. He continued on with their grievances. The prisoners felt that they were badly treated in Bang Kwang and that nobody on the outside really cared about their welfare. They said they were being treated no better than caged animals. They had to take over the prison because no one else was going to help them. The politicians who promised mass amnesty had all but disappeared. Furthermore, if they didn't get amnesty, they would rather die.

At 2.30pm prison officers at Klong Prem Prison were instructed to gather all their spare spotlights and torches and bring them to Bang Kwang. We had to prepare for the fact that the situation was going to continue into the night. Klong Prem was also hosting its Visiting Day and, like us, would have rented out a lot of electrical equipment for the occasion. Some of our officers were appointed official recorders of the proceedings. They were to take photos and film the riot scene. Then we heard a big commotion as a large group from Wing 5 tried to break into Wing 2 for some fresh recruits. One of the guards fired a warning shot from the 7-storey security tower, which sent the group running back to 5.

At 3pm medical staff arrived at the prison. The Ministry of Interior had requested the hospital in Nonthaburi to send over doctors and nurses just in case. Hundreds of onlookers had now gathered at the prison gates to watch the scene unfold. Police had cleared and closed the roads around Bang Kwang for about 3km. The town had come to a stand still. The prisoners became more and more agitated when it seemed that they were not going to get to talk to any of the officials that they had requested meeting. They resumed their chanting of 'No amnesty? We would rather die.' It was hoped that they might start to get bored or realise the fruitlessness of their actions. Then at approximately 4.30pm the Vice-Director-General took a chance and got on the megaphone. He implored the prisoners to stop the riot and return to their cells. In response we heard the ring leaders tell the men to ignore the official request and continue on shouting their demands.

However his words did achieve something. Inmates from Wings 1, 2 and 3 ceased trying to join the others and allowed themselves to be locked back into their cells. The inmates from 4, 5 and 6 were most definitely the reckless ones. They were not going to listen to reason any time soon and kept busy in their attempts to climb the adjoining walls between the three wings. Some of the shackled prisoners—those on death row or those who had broken house rules—were trying to get rid of their chains. They were using crow bars to crack them open. This was to be expected, as no man wants to be shackled—he can't take off his shorts and it's harder to complete his daily routine.

At 4.50pm the Vice-Director-General thought to try his luck again. He had officers install amplifiers at the security tower and he climbed up on to the fort with his megaphone to beseech the rioters to calm down and stop destroying prison property. Again they ignored him, and merely countered his request with a demand for food and drink to be sent to Wing 6.

***

Tew makes another appearance into the story at this point. A few of the women were asked to set up a food stall across the road from the prison to cater for the extra staff and the families who didn't want to leave their loved ones behind until they were sure they were safe. She told me all about it later with great excitement and pride. I'm almost sure that I had to sit through many intricate details about the recipes and ingredients used, and the number of serving plates needed, before she would let me tell her my experiences of the day.

'Some police and prison officers hadn't had a chance to eat lunch so we were frantically cooking our butts off for literally hundreds of uniforms. We also had to feed the officers who were stationed on the security and watch towers. We placed the food in plastic bags and a rope was lowered down from the tower. The bag was tied to the rope and away it went. In the evening the Bang Kwang authorities asked the Por Tek Teung Foundation to give us a hand. They helped us cook rice and simple dishes, and distributed it to the officers and medical staff. We also cooked and packed up food for the prisoners.'

Seven hours had passed now and there was no sign that the riot was subsiding. All day we just urged the prisoners to be calm and reasonable but as the hours passed their arrogance grew. It was very frustrating for the prison guards; we knew all the men and couldn't understand why they were insisting on seeing this to a potentially bitter end. They didn't seem to realise the seriousness of their actions. They booed any of the suits who tried to talk to them. First they would pretend to be listening and nodding in agreement and then some fools at the back would start making farting noises and that would be that. They also had a great laugh making fun of us prison guards. They entertained one another by imitating us giving orders, which cracked them up no end. They even had the neck to bum cigarettes off me when I was sending in their food, which I found exasperating.

They had probably expected us to physically react hours earlier and perhaps they thought that if we hadn't by now we were not going to storm the prison. They were given umpteen chances throughout the day to end their protest but they had refused each time. The Director of the Royal Thai Police was keeping the Prime Minister General Prem Tinsoolanon informed with regular updates. The bosses retired to have another meeting to discuss what to do next.

I was on the seventh floor of the tower and had a perfect view of all the activity outside on the street, and I was starting to fret. There was a huge crowd milling around all abuzz with chat and gesture. I almost wished I could join the party; at least they could just sit back and watch without worry or responsibility.

I could just make out Tew feverishly ladling rice on to plate after plate. She and her colleagues worked at break-neck speed as if they were on a mission. Their sweating faces looked grim but I knew they were probably enjoying every minute of it. The smell of fried food was rife in the air and making me hungry.

Every Thai TV station must have sent out a crew to cover the event. Each team jostled with the crowd to get closest to the entrance, though how they could make themselves heard over the noise was beyond me. The prisoners continued with their megaphone-tirades against Bank Kwang, the prison officers and the politicians. This last one struck a particular chord with the crowd and I watched in horror as the hundreds of onlookers started to nod their heads in agreement and, worse than that, claps their hands in approval.

What on earth was going to happen next? Had we left it too late—should we not have tried to break the riot this morning? If the general public decided to support rioting criminals then our problem had just got severely worse.

It was starting to get dark. The Superintendent told the prison officers that we were not to leave Bang Kwang and asked us to be extra vigilant in case the prisoners attempted an escape under the cover of darkness. I briefly wondered how much this was going to cost the government for all our over-time but I didn't really care if it ran into thousands of baht. It wasn't really my concern. I just wanted it to end peacefully. If I was tired at 10 that morning, I was utterly exhausted now. My back and neck ached and I dreamt about taking a long hot bath. Tew would want one too, I thought to myself, so she'd better be done before I got home, whenever that would be. It had been a hot day and I felt grubby and smelly.

More armed police and officers arrived to station themselves along the prison's wall. An escape attempt appeared almost inevitable at this point; I mean, what else would they want to do? There couldn't be much food left and if they weren't afraid to die for their demands then they would surely think that they might as well try to get out. The biggest worry was that, just beyond the prison wall, were the homes of ordinary people who would be in great danger if any of the hardliners escaped.

Certainly the journalists were getting bored of the status quo and hoped that something else would happen. Some press photographers had climbed into the coconut trees that lined the street. They perched on branches clutching the trunks of their trees and their cameras to their chest. Their chums stood on the ground asking them what they could see. Inmates waved their banners at the cameras and a few of them were trying to engage in dialogue through the windows. Others reporters had climbed onto the roofs of nearby buildings. The gates were covered by the TV cameras—how many people throughout the country were watching my place of work?

At 5.40pm the suits' meeting ended and General Narong Mahanon of the Royal Thai Police approached the pleading TV crews to give an interview. He looked relaxed and confidant.

'The incident is under control. Some of the prisoners are still gathered in their groups. We are looking into their demands but of course a mass amnesty cannot be granted at any old time. It is up to the government and is especially dependent on His Majesty's mercy.'

One of the journalists asked about extra security measures undertaken by the prison. General Narong nodded his head as if to say 'that's a good question', and replied:

'We have a substantial force made up of police officers from the Crime Suppression Division and military police from the Air Force, along with the prison officers, so there are plenty of us'.

Another journalist asked the General had he entered into any negotiations with the prisoners. He shook his head.

'No I haven't but I believe they want to meet the Minister of the Interior, which would be a waste of their time. They should know that he cannot speed up the process of mass amnesty any more than I can.'

The first journalist asked what the plan was if the inmates refused to co-operate and return to their cells. The General smiled gravely.

'That depends on a number of things. But we are prepared for any possible actuality.'

The journalist persisted in his line of questioning, asking what would we do if the prisoners attempted to break out of the prison. The General paused and everyone waited.

'Well, if that were to happen we would not have any choice but to react as firmly as possible for the safety of everyone here.'

Another journalist asked the General if he had any idea how long the riot was going to be allowed to continue. Again the General tried to remain vague and answered simply.

'That depends.'

The journalist then asked if he could identify the ring leaders but the General refused to name the men just yet. He did, however, assure the TV cameras that he knew exactly who they were. When asked if he or the prison staff had had any inclination that a riot was planned he replied, 'Maybe.'

Still hoping for more specific information a journalist asked him if he expected the riot to get worse. The General looked unconcerned as he answered:

'I cannot say if or when it is going to get any worse but what I will say is that we have enough men to suppress the protest. If the situation developed into something we couldn't control—and I doubt that sincerely—we would receive immediate support from the army and the air force.'

Someone else asked if he though that a political motive was behind the protest, to which the General replied with a definite 'no'. To the question of whether the riot would affect future Visiting Days the General said that he hoped not, but that ultimately the decision rested with the Minister of Interior.

***

At 6pm we were joined by dozens more armed police officers and commandos. The officers from the Crime Suppression Division dragged in big boxes of bullets with them. It felt a little like we were going to war.

While this was going on the prisoners in Wing 6 had put up pictures of His and Her Majesty on the wall and gathered together to sing the national anthem. The national anthem is usually played twice a day on the radio throughout Thailand at 8 in the morning and 6 in the evening and everyone stops what they are doing to stand to attention. I assumed the prisoners wanted to prove their loyalty to the Royal Family and their patriotism, but perhaps the words of our anthem held a particular relevance for their situation.

Thailand is the unity of Thai blood and body.
The whole country belongs to the Thai people, maintaining thus far for the Thai.
All Thais intend to unite together.
Thais love peace, but do not fear to fight.
They will never let anyone threaten their independence.
They will sacrifice every drop of their blood to contribute to the nation; will serve their country with pride and prestige-full of victory.

Later on Sanid Rujinarong, Director-General of the DOC, also gave an interview. The public had to acknowledge that we were doing our utmost for a peaceful outcome. Also, the prisoners had a TV in their wing so it was a prime opportunity to make a subtle appeal to them. Mr Rujinarong told the journalists:

'I have met the prisoner's elected representative. They want amnesty but I have explained that this demand cannot be immediately met. There are a lot of steps involved in an amnesty request. However I have passed on their request to the Minister of Interior so it is his decision to make.'

When he was asked for more information about the riot he obliged, 'There are over two thousand inmates partaking in this riot. We believe that over 80% of these have been pressured into joining it out of fear. Possible only 200 inmates are serious rioters and these would be probably the prison's worst offenders.'

He gave a press conference afterwards at the Visiting Day administrative centre which was opposite Klong Prem prison and stated that the protest and disobedience would only be tolerated until the following day. He was disappointed in the inmates' behaviour and felt that they were not really in a position to be making demands. He also was not happy with their choice of representative. He continued by emphasising the tolerance shown by the authorities up to now, which nobody could argue against.

'So far the media has witnessed how well the DOC has treated the inmates despite their inciting and pushing us to strike back. We have provided them with the chance to rehabilitate and clean up their act. They can better themselves through our distance education program with Sukhothai Thammathirat University in Nonthaburi and through our vocation training program. And this is how they repay us. They are fed and clothed and protected from themselves. Not everyone is lucky enough to get a second chance.'

The man was visibly pissed off.

Back at the prison we had cut off the electricity into the troubled wings. When it got dark, the inmates built small bonfires which they sat around and then sang songs to one another. It was if they thought they were out camping in the woods for a weekend. Did they really know what they were getting themselves into? Was any one of them stopping to wonder about the possible consequences of all of this? I suppose if they weren't allowing themselves to look too far ahead, this would have been a welcome break in the tedium that is a prisoner's lot in life. The rioters included the worst graded inmates and they did not share the same freedom as the others. Not only could they not receive visitors but they were not allowed to walk around Bang Kwang. Keeping angry men cooped up all day against their will creates a pressure point which is waiting to explode. Only the inmates at Wing 4 were permitted to leave their wing daily to work in the vocational training area.

It was completely dark at 9pm; I couldn't see my hand in front of my face. A large truck with spotlights was driven into the prison ground to help the officers' visibility. About an hour later there was a black Mercedes at the prison gates—Veera Musikpong, the Deputy Minister of Interior had arrived. Another meeting with just the officials was called.

On his way out of the prison he stopped to answer a few questions. He was very businesslike and told the cameras:

'Everything is now under control. The protesters have scattered and are no longer making any trouble.'

When he was asked how he thought the riot was going to end he replied that he had absolute confidence in the officers to handle the situation. There was no need for him to involve himself any further in personally addressing the prisoners. He echoed the other interviewees by saying that the amnesty process was a lengthy one so there was no point in creating all this trouble. He hoped that the situation would soon be resolved; however, he warned that if it wasn't, the officers had a job to do, which meant ending the riot as quickly and definitely as possible. The prisoners were to take from his words—if they were watching—that this wouldn't be the best option for them.

We next turned off the water to Wings 4, 5 and 6. It didn't seem to have any obvious effect. The inmates appeared to be having a big party and continued in their clambering across the adjoining walls, shouting and whooping like crazy people. They obviously were not as tired as I was. Frisking the relatives that morning seemed like an eternity ago. It was almost midnight and I was sure that it was just a matter of time before we made our move. I have to say that I wondered at the leniency shown to the rioters. I might not have tolerated them for this long had I been in charge, but then Tew has always accused me of being too hasty. I was angry now; these trouble-makers were preventing me from being at home with my family. The job was tough enough without this. The prisoners did not understand that they were not in a position to make demands of our government officials. This was not the way to promote healthy dialogue. Protesting for a mass amnesty was one thing; wantonly breaking house rules was another thing entirely. All it did was piss the superiors off, they would never achieve anything this way. They had refused to enter into proper negotiations with any of my superiors, so intent were they on seeing the Minister of Interior. Surely they knew that if we couldn't talk to them we had only one other alternative. If I wasn't so mad at them I might have felt sorry for them and their ignorance. I did truly hope that there wouldn't be a bloody ending—but time was running out.

At midnight the Superintendent told some of the officers to fetch more spotlights and point them at the walls of Wing 6 and also at the security tower and outer wall. An officer had been sent out earlier to buy 15 lengths of rope which was then quickly cut up into smaller ropes of one metre long—homemade handcuffs. I just hoped we had enough. It was hard to be sure. When we broke in the number of protesters might undergo a radical change, with either a major increase as they united together or a massive decrease when confronted with armed guards, police and commandos. Three fire-fighting trucks arrived on the scene and were directed to park near Wings 4, 5 and 6. As I was also in charge of the prison clinic I was ordered by the Superintendent to take some of the police officers and station them on the second floor to prevent any inmates from 1, 2 and 3 from trying to escape. The clinic separated these three wings from the temple and as the temple was not a fortress of bars and locks, it was probably the weakest point on the prison grounds. If you got to the clinic undetected you would just have to scale the outer wall to freedom.

As we headed to the clinic a busybody inmate from Wing 1 spotted me and the armed officers through a window and started yelling to the others: 'It's the cops—and they're armed!'

I rolled my eyes upwards and said to the officers, 'Here we go.'

As I expected, the sick prisoners in the clinic were suddenly able to raise a raucous. If the prison staff were unpopular with the prisoners the police were really hated, as they were the ones who had put them in prison. A chorus of boos and cat calls filled the air, accompanied by the banging of chairs against bars. The police officers managed to look either bored or deaf. After a few minutes I decided I wasn't having this and yelled out that if they didn't shut up I was going to send their sick asses into Wing 6. It worked and most of them went back to sleep. I suppose they just felt they had to make a point, and by then they would have guessed that Wing 6 was soon to become a battlefield and sensibly preferred to stay in their sick bed.

Since nobody on the ground knew just yet what the suits were planning, rumours were flying back and forth between the police, prison staff and the army. It was a relief to be doing something at last and we were all on our second wind. The adrenaline was starting to build like it does before any fight. The most prevalent rumour was that Bang Kwang authorities were going to use the police force to charge the rioters at maybe 6am or 9am the following morning. Whatever the time, the protest was going to be over by noon.

At 12.30am the Superintendent upgraded all the police officers present to that of special warden. This meant that they now had the same power as that of a prison officer—they could shoot prisoners, if necessary. The inmates could be shot under three circumstances. Firstly, if a prisoner refuses to drop his weapon after he has been ordered to. Secondly, if a prisoner was trying to escape and didn't stop after he had been told to. And thirdly, if three or more prisoners were attempting to open the prison gate, or if they were caught destroying prison property, or if they were assaulting officers or other prisoners—and even then they were only to be shot if they refused to stop what they were doing. However, shooting was not to take place unless the guard had received the go-ahead from a superior officer. This wasn't a war; shooting was to be the last resort. The inmates were to be given the opportunity to stop whatever it was they were doing—it wasn't like a Rambo movie, act first then talk later.

In Wing 6 the majority of the rioters were asleep after their long day. Just the leaders were still awake and discussing their strategies for the next morning. The prison officers used the break to practice with the nylon ropes; how best to tie it as fast and effectively as possible. The quiet didn't last too long, as the singing and chanting began again around 2am. The rumour was confirmed that the strike would happen at 9am. It was perfect timing as the prisoners would be drowsy from lack of sleep and looking for their breakfast. We were to nab the ring leaders first, handcuff them with the rope and bring them straight to the solitary confinement cells. I managed to grab a few hours sleep myself. I was starting to see double at this point and knew if I didn't close my eyes I would be useless the next day.

At 3.20am the inmates at Wing 5 joined with Wing 6 in hollering insults and throwing things from the windows. A couple of hours later no less than six fire-fighting trucks arrived; two entered the prison grounds while the others remained just outside the entrance. Both sides were busy with their preparations. The inmates gathered together all the bamboo, used to make furniture in the prison workshop, they could find, and started to sharpen it into spears and clubs.

At 7am the Governor of Nonthaburi and a deputy from the Minister of Interior arrived for the first meeting of the day. The inmates were aware that the officials had returned. They wrote a few letters, attached them to rocks and flung them down into the grounds. Some officers collected them and brought them to the attention of the Superintendent. One of the notes was as follows;

Wrote at Wing 5,
5 August 1985

Subject: Bang Kwang Inmates' Request
Attention: The Government

No. 1: We want the government to arrange mass amnesty for us on the occasion of Her Majesty's birthday on 12 August 1985. (Announcement about the amnesty must be publicised by the National Public Relations' Department and in the presence of the media.)

No.2: The DOC must not punish us for this protest.

No.3: The Ministry of Interior must guarantee that there will be no penalty both in legal terms and house rules.

No.4. Give us your answer within three hours of receiving this letter or else we inmates will be forced to act accordingly.

We sincerely hope we will be granted justice as requested.

Best regards,
The inmates of Bang Kwang

Poor bastards!

At 7.30am the Director-General of the Royal Thai Police ordered the commandoes to prepare the tear gas for the strike. The megaphone was used again to ask the prisoners to end their protest peacefully and return to their cells, but the inevitable happened. All the locks on the cell doors were damaged and the prisoners who tried to obey the Superintendent were blocked from returning to their quarters. Instead they were handed weapons and threatened with death if they didn't participate in the riot. They were the ones I felt most sorry for. Another letter was sent advising the authorities that the prison would be set on fire in three hours if they didn't receive a favourable response to their request.

At 7.40am the protesters promised to stay calm and begged for food and water. The inmates in Wings 1, 2 and 3 were very quiet. They could see more from where they were and probably better understood just how many officers were located around the prison and how well armed we were. At 8am the national anthem rang out clearly as the protesters sang it loudly to impress upon us their patriotism, as if that would deter us from attacking them.

The media was buzzing with reports that there had been a battle during the night resulting in 500 prisoners in need of medical aid at the prison clinic. I don't know who made that one up. But just after 8am, 20 more military police arrived with Uzi guns. Wing 2's inmates were suddenly filled with a zeal for the underdog and starting hurling stones at the roofs of Wing 1 and 3 telling them to join the others in protest.

Some relatives arrived, oblivious to all the trouble, wishing to visit their loved one. I don't know how they hadn't heard about what was going on. A sign was placed at the entrance declaring that visiting hours would be cancelled for the next 15 days. The crowd at the front gate starting to increase in number and anticipation. The last wing to join the protest was Wing 1, the wing that housed the criminals on death row. Then, at about 8.30am they started to destroy prison facilities and climb across the walls to 1 and 3, brandishing weapons. I always wondered why they waited so long to join in. They had already lost everything. Perhaps they were past hoping and didn't see the point, and more importantly, the amnesty would have meant nothing to them. The prison was in a bad state by now. Most of the offices and workshops had been damaged and stripped of equipment.

Just before 9am the first shot was fired, from the security tower. Rioters had run into the canteen in Wing 6 to take cover. An inmate was trying to dismantle the roof of his cell and the officer fired a warning shot, which startled him. He fell off the roof in fright.

It was Noi Gitsuwan, one of the ring leaders. The fall wasn't big enough to kill him but he was hurt and unable to get to his feet. Some of his friends picked him up and carried him around the wing declaring him to have been shot. This angered their cell mates and they threatened to burn down the wing in response to this terrible shooting. They weren't lying.

At 9.30am inmates in Wing 3 and 4 set fire to their respective workshops. Smoke could be seen escaping to the sky. Fortunately the more sensible inmates extinguished the fires before they could cause much damage. The men were next told to bring flammable substances and fuel to the factory in Wing 6. Another of the ring leaders, Jumroon Intanon, led his fellow protesters in setting fire to the factory in Wing 6. Smoke bellowed out of the windows. One of the fire-fighting trucks shot water across the top of the wing but it was no use, the factory was too far in. We couldn't afford to lose the wing so we were very pleased indeed when a few prisoners approached the nearest fire truck to them and told the fire-fighters to throw the water hose across the wall to them. Jane Katigumjorn and his friends took the hose and immediately set about putting out the fire. After the riot, Jane and his mates were promoted to 'assistants' in gratitude for their help that morning.

At 10am the Director-General of the Royal Thai Police got on the phone to ask for more reinforcements. As a result, within 30 minutes, Montri Chomsakorn, the Police Inspector of the SWAT team, arrived in Bang Kwang with 40 officers. Another meeting was called between the suits. There were so many different groups of forces around the prison grounds they had to make sure that we were all working in sync with one another and knew what we were doing. The plan had changed again. 20 minutes later we heard that the SWAT and Commandoes were going to lead the strike against the prisoners. I assumed that the starting of fires had just worsened the consequences for the rioters. I was ordered along with a couple of prison colleagues to lead the SWAT and Commandoes in. They had been ordered to start 'cleaning up'. Most of these guys had never been in a prison before and it is a big place when you see it for the first time. Only the SWAT, Commandoes and some police officers were allowed to use their guns. The rest of us were to stand by, ready. We would wait to see the reaction that the others got.

At 10.45am the two armed teams entered Wing 4 in a single file. They constantly fired their guns in the air to make as much noise as possible, causing a big distraction and letting the rioters know that we meant business. As was hoped, there was absolutely no resistance. The inmates started to fall back immediately. The elder inmates were so shocked that they stood still, unable to move. They had not participated in the riot, preferring to sit together away from the younger inmates. They had to be pushed and dragged by their wing mates. The guns continued firing, probably for the benefit of the other two wings, 5 and 6, where it was felt a stronger resistance would be waiting. Within 30 minutes the inhabitants of Wing 4 had completely surrendered, which meant that the prison chiefs were back in the fold.

The SWAT team assembled the inmates outside in front of their quarters and instructed them to drop their weapons on the ground so that they could be piled together in the centre. Then they were told to remove their shirts and lie face down on the ground with their hands behind their backs. Some of them were told to dismantle the pyramid of table and chairs, making them first line up to be frisked. The prison officers who looked after Wing 4 re-established themselves at their posts and took over to let the SWATs and Commandoes continue on to the next wing.

The officer leading the two teams thought that all the commotion might have scared the men in 5 and 6 into giving up their futile fight, so he wanted to give them a final opportunity to co-operate. He sent for the megaphone and told these inmates in 5 that he wished the riot to end as peacefully and orderly as possible, reminding them that how it ended was completely up to themselves.

'We would ask you to do the following: first drop your weapons, come outside to front of your sleeping quarters, and remove your shirts. Second I need you to lie face down on the ground and place your hands at the back of your necks. Lastly I want you to know that after we have searched every individual you will be sent back to your cells where you will be supplied with food and water. If you do not comply with my instructions we have no alternative but to deal with you in a forceful matter. I sincerely hope that it doesn't come to that'.

Above our heads two Thai army helicopters circled the prison, ready to help.

Well, I must admit that I, for one, was very surprised when the inmates booed back their response and I'm certainly not naïve after all my years working in the prison. The noise from Wing 4 would have had me running scared if I was a prisoner in 5 and 6. I heard afterwards that a lot of people out on the streets assumed that the prisoners were dying in their hundreds when they heard the volume of gun fire. However, maybe the booing was all for show for the TV cameras and onlookers. When the armed forces moved into Wing

5 and started shooting up another racket the inmates surrendered without a fuss. It took even less time and effort than Wing 4.

The megaphone was used again with the same request for Wing 6. At 11.45am the armed teams moved in and started shooting into the sky for effect. Most of the inmates there surrendered. They were told to sit and wait by the factory that they almost succeeded in burning down. There were a couple of complications with this wing so it was decided to push on to the first three wings and end their belated and half-hearted rebellion. In less than 40 minutes Wings 1, 2 and 3 were back to normal without any trouble. I really think it was just a break in routine for these particular wings but they knew that nothing was going to come of it.

Back to Wing 6. We knew that seven armed convicts were hiding out in the attack of Wing 6. I was to lead the SWAT and Commando teams upstairs. The convicts were trying to set fire to some mattresses and black smoke drifted out through the cracks in the roof. This prompted the teams to act quickly as we certainly did not want any unnecessary deaths on our hands, or the loss of a precious wing. Our superiors had plenty to be concerned about. If a man died during the riot at this point the blame might easily fall on us, whether it was because his cell mate burnt down the prison or not. The media were watching. A riot had to be contained but we also had to be conscious of the prison's image that was being transported into the nation's homes via TV cameras. 24 cells on the first floor were swiftly cleared. We would have been badly stuck for space if anyone had succeeded in burning down a wing that day. The prison was already over-crowded enough as it was.

Just as I stepped onto the last stair, I noticed some footprints on the wall to my right, in cell 37. There was a small door on the ceiling which electricians used to reach the wires in the attics. The lock on this door was broken so it was obvious that the prisoners had used this door to get into the loft. The head of the team gave a silent signal, sending two armed officers to quietly check all the cells on the second floor. They returned giving us the all clear. The leader muttered into his walkie talkie, asking for a ladder to be brought up. Just seconds later, one of the electricians appeared, smiling nervously, with a bamboo ladder which was placed against the wall by the attic door. He fled the tense room and I was waved aside out of harm's way.

The same two guys who had checked the cells were sent again to walk the corridor between the cells. This time they fired their weapons into the ceiling as they walked up and down. It was like something from an Arnold Schwarzenegger movie. Within seconds of the shooting I distinctly heard footsteps moving rapidly over our heads. Suddenly there was a crash as one of the inmates fell through the ceiling into the corridor. The floor of the attic was made of wood that was old and rotting. It had just given way. I had initially thought that he had been shot. While I had turned to see him land on the ground the rest of the team had charged up the ladder and there was a terrible commotion as the guns just kept shooting. The noise was deafening.

The one who fell raised his hands in the air and begged the officers not to shoot him. He was trembling all over and when I looked in his eyes I saw the fear that is in the eyes of every prisoner on death row when they realise that their time is up. The SWAT guy handcuffed him and asked him how many were still upstairs. Seven was the reply. Just then there was silence above and the head of the SWAT team shouted, 'Cleared'. It was over. I knew that this meant there were seven dead men in the attic but I just couldn't bring myself to climb the ladder to see for myself.

This might sound strange coming from an executioner but it goes to show that I had no interest in blood and gore for its own sake. Like most people I shied away from climbing that ladder just to gawk at seven dead men. Instead I moved gingerly around the cells, offices and workshop, checking out the damage done.

A lot of furniture had been destroyed, especially in the fire in the factory/workshop. There was also a small flood in the factory. There were plastics bags full of shit and piss in the alley of the cell building, since the toilets had run out of water the previous night. They had also served as obstacles to officers entering. Needless to say the place stank worse than usual. The offices had been almost destroyed, with the furniture removed, papers strewn everywhere and documents set on fire. The vegetable plot was a mess, the whole area looked like a war zone, but at least the situation was under control again.

Soon after, representatives from the Italian and American embassies arrived to check on their nationals. However, no foreign prisoners had been harmed and they only stayed for about an hour. They would have taken worried phone calls from the families in their respective countries and would have had to personally check it out. Certainly there was no point in trying to ring Bang Kwang as most of the phones had been pulled out of their sockets and we were just too busy to be answering phones anyway. The extra forces started to pull out at about 2.30pm. The SWATs and Commandoes were the first to leave. I shook the hands of the guys I had been dealing with and they wished me luck with the restoration job. They didn't envy my job one little bit.

That evening, at about 5pm the Director-General held a press conference.

'Everything is now under control. The SWAT and Commando teams advanced into Wings 4, 5 and 6. The leaders in Wing 6 attempt to resist. They had armed themselves from the prison workshop. They also tried to set the building on fire. Therefore we had to use force and, as a result, seven inmates died. We believe that 50 inmates were responsible for starting this riot and they are currently being kept in solitary confinement. A full investigation is being undertaken and a penalty will be meted out to these inmates according to their contribution to the protest. We estimate that the damage to the prison is in the region of 7 million baht.'

A journalist asked what was happening to these inmates in the meantime and he replied; 'Well, we are feeding them and making sure they have plenty of water. They were all very hungry. The inmates who look after the cooking for the prison are housed in Wing 4 and once that wing decided to get involved in the protest they didn't do any more cooking.'

Another journalist asked about the rumour that a lot of prisoners had hung themselves when the armed forces moved in. The Director-General replied that he hadn't seen any evidence of this yet.

'As far as I'm concerned we had to use force. Therefore any resisting prisoners were going to be shot. This use of force had the approval of a committee which consisted of the Director of the Metropolitan Prison Guard Force, the Deputy Minister of Interior and the Director-General of the Royal Thai Police, and myself, of course.'

Afterwards a couple of members of the SWAT team gave an interview and said that three inmates were found hanging in the attic of Wing 6. They had died from their own hands since the armed forces would never kill someone in this way.

***

Normal visiting resumed within a week. The prison made that a priority because we understand how important visits are for the relatives, as well as the inmates. The inmates and officers worked together to fix the broken machinery and furniture and all in all it took about a month to complete the repairs. We used money generated from within the prison, like the shop, and also applied for some money from the government. The biggest interior decorating consequence was that the tables in the canteen were set into cement and covered with stones—there would be no more pyramids built with their help ever again.

The 50 prisoners deemed responsible had to wear leg irons and they were left in solitary confinement for three months. They were lucky, it could have been worse—at the very least landing back in court before a strict judge. The Superintendent decided to show them mercy and spared them any further punishment. Section 317 of the Correction Act entitled the Superintendent to let a prisoner go relatively unpunished if the prisoner commits certain types of offences—like vandalising prison property, a minor physical assault or carrying cash. He explained that if they went to court they could be downgraded, which would mean they wouldn't have a hope in hell for the next Royal Pardon. So you see we do have a heart! That evening I was disappointed to see some of the police officers slap a few of the inmates about the head. The prison staff would never indulge in that kind of behaviour, especially when dealing with prisoners who are chained and subdued. There is just no need for it.

It was the officers in charge of each wing who frisked the rest of the inmates after they surrendered. As there was more than a few thousand this took a while.

There were plenty of weapons to confiscate, though we were assured by more than one guy that the weapons were mostly about protecting themselves from other inmates—the men weren't as unified as they had appeared to the media and us. The usual suspects took advantage of the chaos to continue and expand the usual power struggles. Some men just need to always be fighting.

The prisoners began to feed the officers information as to who was involved in the riot and who did what. Quite a few of these inmates, now happy to redeem themselves and return to our good books, offered to help with an initial clean-up that evening. They followed our orders and directions without a whimper. I think we were all as tired as each other. I certainly could have done with a few days off but we were too short staffed and the Superintendent really wanted things to return to complete normality. My kids thought they were never going to see me again. They hadn't seen me in two days and I got a great reception when I finally returned home for a few hours sleep before my next shift.

Three months might seem like a long time to leave the men in solitary confinement but we had to be seen to take their disobedience seriously. Although several of them told me that they preferred solitary confinement to living in the wings—each man has his own toilet in his cell and it would have been a relief to have some time to be alone. They could also relax as they were safe from gang fights and bad-tempered bullies. However, they couldn't get too lonely as they could still hold conversations with their immediate neighbours. When the 50 returned to their wings there were no hard feelings between them and the staff, and life just continued on as normal. Thankfully, that was the last riot in the prison.

Not surprisingly, Bang Kwang and Klong Prem cancelled their Visiting Day, which was a great pity for all those inmates who benefited from the day and never caused any trouble. Tew was not too happy either as it meant the end to her working away from the home. The kids and I had been at her to give up the food stall and she compromised by telling us that she would when the prison didn't need her anymore. It had been a bit of extra money for us but I much preferred knowing that she was at home for the kids.

CHAPTER 13

Executions were always worse when the condemned was a woman.

Samai Pan-in was charged with drug offences and sentenced to the death penalty on 5 June 1998. She had built up quite a criminal record, with 12 previous charges and her final arrest was the last straw for the authorities. Her death took place on 30 June 1994 when she was picked up by officers from the Narcotics Control Board. Six people were arrested that day after police had been watching a house in the Bangken district of Bangkok that was known to be central to a local drug smuggling operation. Prasert Piyaranga bought heroin from Somporn and delivered it to Somjai Thong-O, the woman of the house in Bangkok.

On the day of her arrest, Somjai's daughter rang Pan-in to tell her that Somjai wanted to see her. However, when Pan-in reached the woman's house she wasn't there. A neighbour told her that she was visiting her daughter so Pan-in hitched a ride to the daughter's house. The doors and windows were closed and Somjai walked around it to see whether mother or daughter was about. As she approached the front of the house a man stopped her to ask who she was looking for. When she told him that she was looking for Somjai he revealed himself to be a plain clothes police officer and showed her his badge. He proceeded to search her and found 130,000 baht in her bag, in 1,000 baht banknotes. The officer asked her why she was carrying so much money and she told him that Somjai was going to borrow the money to buy a flat, as her house had recently burnt down.

Several more officers appeared and she was escorted into the house and up the stairs to where Somjai and her family, Malee, Den and Aroonsak were pouring heroin into plastic tubes. The police had told them to pose specially for photographs. They had already confessed everything to the police. 14-year-old Den, a neighbourhood boy who was hired to help pour the heroin into tubes and sometimes distribute it, had disclosed his helping out and he confirmed Pan-in's involvement. He was sent to a young offender's correction centre. His father had already been arrested for drug smuggling a few years before but because he couldn't handle life in Bang Kwang he committed suicide by hanging himself in 1991. His sister Malee was sentenced to 50 years in prison and his other sister Aroonsak was sentenced to life imprisonment along with his mother Somjai. What a family! Pan-in denied all charges and was denied bail. She was sent to the Central Women's Correctional Institution in Lard Yao to await her trial.

Further investigation uncovered how the gang bought heroin from a drug lord in the north of Thailand. They usually procured between 15 to 20 bags at a time and then the heroin was poured into tubes, which took some time but was something that a child could help with. Pan-in would then bring the tubes to dealers in the Klongtoey slum community. She had been doing this for so long that she was well-known and had her own special name, 'Lady Mafia of Block 4'. Officers had been watching the 53-year-old for sometime now. She was skinny and just over five feet tall, with short dark hair, and constantly maintained innocence of any drug-dealing. She stubbornly fought her case through three different courts until 5 June 1998 when the Supreme (Dika) Court found her guilty and handed out the death penalty. She had 60 days to submit her petition for amnesty, which was subsequently rejected over a year later on 26 October 1999.

It was rejected because of her 12 previous arrests, which proved to the courts that she had no respect for the law, and also because her testimony was found to be based on lies. Therefore, on 23 November 1999, Prime Minister Chuan Leekpai informed the Interior Ministry to direct Sawat Songsampan, Director-General of the Department of Corrections, to carry out the death sentence as Pan-in's petition had been rejected. The following morning at about 10.30am the execution team and I were told that we would be executing a female. There were also two other executions lined up that day. Tapoyho was charged with illegal immigration and with carrying out a violent murder. Prayuth Polpan was sentenced for being an accomplice to a murder, attempting another murder and for being in possession of an illegal fire-arm.

These two were already seated side by side when Pan-in arrived at Bang Kwang in a police van around 3pm. Six female officers from the female prison escorted the trembling woman to her seat. She didn't fully understand what was happening. She glanced around at the other convicts and at our own prison staff. A small crowd had gathered because of her sex and notoriety. After a few minutes she breathlessly asked the nearest female officer why she had been brought here. The officer looked genuinely upset.

'We were ordered to bring you and your papers to Bang Kwang but we weren't told why. But we have just been informed a few minutes ago that you are to be executed here today.'

Pan-in burst into tears. The convict Prayuth who was sitting next to her was touched by her tears.

'Don't cry', he said, 'Tapoyho and me are going to be executed too. We did wrong and now it's pay back time. What did you do?'

Through her sobs she gasped, 'White powder. But I really didn't think I was going to be executed.' She continued to weep into her hands.

One of our officers intervened.

'Sister, the other officers and I have to do our job. I am deeply sorry for you but there's nothing that can help you now. Please stop crying and try to gather yourself together.'

She tried to catch her breath and asked the officer if she could have a word with her daughter. He shook his head sadly, 'I'm sorry but you are forbidden to use the telephone at this point. Though, when they have taken your fingerprints you will be provided with a pen and paper. That's the best we can do.'

She pleaded that it would just take a few minutes but he explained that it was out of his hands, that only the Superintendent or a superior officer from the DOC could authorise her to use the phone.

At 4.30pm an officer arrived from the Criminal Record Department along with three female officers. Pan-in begged them to call her daughter as they took her photograph and fingerprints. Nobody met her eye or headed for the phone. Then she was taken away to change from her skirt into trousers. On her return she wrote her letter. She was an uneducated woman who had led a tough life and her blunt letter lacked warmth and sentiment;

'Kids, stay away from drugs. Take me as an example of what not to do. All the money I made from drugs I spent on the trial. It's not worth it. I must say goodbye now.'

One of the female officers helped her to compose it and she wrote slowly while constantly dabbing her eyes with a tissue.

The execution order was read to the three convicts. Only Pan-in showed any emotion, the other two stared at the ground, utterly resigned. No one ate their last meal. They just sipped their water quietly. Pan-in appeared cried out at this stage and she asked for a glass of alcohol. The escorts smiled kindly and said no. He offered her a cup of coffee instead. She shrugged.

'No this, no that! You know, you guys could show a little mercy to me for the last time.'

Eventually she accepted the coffee and even a cigarette. A little while later she ate an orange that one of the female officers gave her.

Then it was time for the last rites. Two female officers lifted Pan-in up by both her arms and brought her to the abbot. The officers looked worse off than their charge. They were visibly sweating and their hands had a slight tremor. They had obviously never escorted anyone to the execution room before. Pan-in was to be the first that evening and the two guards looked in confusion at each other. Pan-in was the only person who was oblivious to their discomfort. As they made to bring her over one of the Bang Kwang guys lightly touched one of them on the arm and asked if he could take over. The women smiled in thanks and relief, and quickly stepped aside. Two men took their place.

To ease the usual tension, one of the escorts joked with Pan-in and asked her would she permit him to be her last boyfriend? She giggled and asked how he could love such an old woman as herself who was also a prisoner. She linked her arm with his and stretched up to plant a kiss on his cheek. The officers and witnesses who followed behind applauded her actions and new-found composure. She beamed at their appreciation.

At the gazebo she was blindfolded and placed on a chair unshackled. Female prisoners are never shackled. At 5.40pm she was tied to the cross without a struggle or a sound out of her. She had adjusted herself to her fate and was ready. When Rangsan Muangjareon let down the red flag I shot seven bullets in to her. She was dead at 5.45pm. I counted and picked the seven shells up from the floor and shouted 'clear' to the others to let them know that they could bring in the two men. At 6.13pm 13 shots killed Prayuth by my hand while Topoyho was shot simultaneously by the second gun. The other executioner that day was my unfortunate colleague Prayuth Sanan, the officer who is currently awaiting trial on death row.

Pan-in was divorced with one son and two daughters. She and her children lived with her sister. Her son was unemployed while her daughters were students. Everyone thought she made her money from selling second-hand clothes in the flea markets. I was told her sad story over the dinner that the team shared after the executions. Gomol Yimpenyai from the Criminal Record Department of the Royal Thai Police explained how she was involved in international drug smuggling, something that she had steadfastly refused to admit. As I have already said drug-crime is taken very seriously in Thailand, more so after 12 previous arrests. Perhaps Pan-in could have supported her family selling clothes in the markets, but she chose another route and became only the third, and last ever woman to be executed by gun in Thailand. She risked everything for her kids and consequently deprived them of something essential they needed the most—her.

CHAPTER 14

One of the most difficult aspects of facing an execution is the waiting. It must be torture for most of the condemned; knowing they will soon die, but not knowing exactly when. Their fate looms over them like a shadow of death, and their every waking moment must be filled with anxiety. The waiting must seem to go on forever, but will never last long enough, before, with a sudden burst of fire, it is all over.

It is something removed from normal life, where thekilling of another person is never set to strict rules and protocol. From the cases that I have seen, and the people I have put to death, I have learned that in the world at large, someone's life can be taken away so suddenly, without warning, or ceremony. This is a disturbing thought.

One case in particular, later in my career, highlighted this fact to me and showed just how quickly death can come.

***

At around 4am on the morning of 18 August 1998, Athip Ingaew and his wife Ganya were already at work, collecting latex from the trees on a rubber farm. The early morning is the best time to collect the rubber because the temperature is much more suitable. The rubber trees will release white latex then, which is considered the best quality rubber of all. The husband and wife were working on separate rows, scraping each tree and attaching a little cup to the trunk to collect the precious commodity. The farm belonged to another couple, Niyom and Pen Kongtago, and was situated in the province of Chumporn. In the twilight Ganya heard a sound and looked up in surprise. She could just make out the approaching figure of a man. He was nearer to Athip and she quietly called to her husband. When he turned around to face the man the visitor produced a gun and aimed it at Athip. Before the couple could respond, Ganya watched her husband fall to his knees as a single shot rang out, sounding vulgar in an otherwise peaceful scene. Forgetting herself, Ganya screamed out and ran to her husband who had crumpled down to the ground and was now motionless. The assailant was about three metres away as Ganya reached Athip and she found herself peering at him against her better judgement. The sun had not risen yet but she could make out his face in the light from the small lamp attached to her helmet.

With her husband's head in her lap she recoiled in horror from the monster with the gun—a monster that she knew well. It was Sudjai, her step-father. Sudjai, the bastard who had raped her over a period of five years. Sudjai, the father of her aborted child. He had made her life a misery and it was Athip who had rescued her from the abuse. He held the gun rigidly by his side and stared coldly at her.

'If you tell the police I will come back and kill you.'

Then he ran off in the direction he had come. Ganya tried to drag her badly wounded husband to the Kongtago house but his weight was too much for her. She didn't know at the time that the shot, at such close range, had killed him, and she frantically tried to rouse him to consciousness, refusing to consider the obvious. She eventually left him to run to the farm owners for help. They called the police and Athip's parents.

Athip's mother reached her first and spent a distressing hour with her sobbing daughter-in-law. At that stage Ganya did not identify her husband's killer, which caused complications later. She just described how her husband had been shot by a man, both to the Kontagos and her mother-in-law. There were a couple of discrepancies, it was later argued, between what she said happened now and what she later said to the police. She said that she saw a man approaching from ten metres away and could not make out his face as it was too dark. She also said that she was collecting latex at the second row of trees while her husband was working at the first row, right next to the mangosteen farm. She insisted that she saw the man coming from the direction of the mangosteen farm, but how could she be sure if she couldn't see that far? The farm was more than 15 metres away from where she was working.

Later that day Ganya was interviewed at the police station and confirmed that the killer was her step-father. The police applied for a search warrant from Langusan Provincial Court, which was quickly issued. They rushed to Sudjai's house that same day but he wasn't there. His wife informed them that he was away working in the district of Langsuan. A warrant was issued for his arrest and six days later they finally caught up with him. He was hiding on a farm in the small village of Pato, and was duly arrested. He denied the two charges put to him, that of cold-blooded murder and being in possession if an illegal firearm.

He also told police: 'I didn't rape the girl. Some guy kills her husband and I'm just the scapegoat.' But then again, raping your step-daughter is hardly something a man is going to admit to.

Ganya told the police everything. She shared a house with her mother and Sudjai for 15 years. After ten years had elapsed Sudjai returned home drunk one day. His wife had gone to Bangkok to do some shopping so he raped his 15-year-old step-daughter instead. After doing it once he found it easier to do it again, and again, and again. She got pregnant and at her mother's instigation she had an abortion. Her step-father resumed raping her after the abortion. Then in April 1997 she fled her home to marry Athip, without her step-father's approval.

She claimed that the light on her helmet allowed her to see 15 metres in front of her. When she saw the killer's face he was only three metres away from her so she was 100 % sure it was Sudjai. He spoke to her and threatened to kill her if she didn't keep her mouth shut.

Aside from the whole matter of how many metres she could see ahead of her in the twilight the police pondered about some other little matters. It was thought to be strange behaviour that she had run to her husband after he had been shot, despite the killer only being three metres away. People believed that had they been in her shoes they would have run to save themselves first. But the way I saw it was that she loved her husband, so it was a natural reaction to forget herself and run to him when he fell. If Tew or any of my kids were attacked in that way I would not run off for cover and leave them lying on the ground behind me, and if it was me that fell they probably wouldn't leave me either. So I was never convinced that this was a controversial matter. And there was another case where a father out walking with his daughter was shot by an assassin, his daughter clung to him and refused to run and consequently was also shot.

They also could not understand why she didn't identify the killer immediately. It was over an hour before the police reached the farm and that is when she used Sudjai's name for the first time. I don't see anything strange in this. Athip was probably the only person that knew what Ganya had been subjected to by her step-dad. How was she to tell her shocked and severely distraught mother-in-law that she was indirectly the cause of her son's death? That her step-father had raped her for five years when she was a teenager and was so obsessed with her that he sought her out to kill her son in jealousy. She was still in shock herself and would have been trying to digest the fact that her own mother's husband had just killed the one person in the world that truly cared about her. She was right to wait for the objectivity and professional calm of the police.

Ganya claimed that Sudjai was mad at her for marrying Athip, but if that was the case why did it take him a year to do something? So what? He didn't think about murdering someone immediately—instead he took a year out to brood and nurture his wicked obsession to the point where he could pick up a gun and hunt out Ganya's young husband to terminate his life. He wasn't a natural born killer; he had to work himself up to it. When I saw photographs of him later he looked like a mad man, very emaciated with a head of short grey hair. His life had probably just consisted of tedious hard labour and hard drinking to make him forget how miserable his life was. He obviously didn't care for his wife so the only other thing is his life was Ganya and he had become fixated on her and never got over her running away from his forced embrace to marry and sleep with another man.

There was also a bit of a problem over the fact that the police searched his house and failed to find the gun or bullets, but why would the guy bring the gun back to his home and risk incriminating himself? Surely he would have gotten rid of the gun following the shooting; he would have been stupid to have done otherwise.

His wife was interviewed by a social worker afterwards for the official report. The day before the murder Sudjai told her that he was going away for a while to work on a farm. That would have been completely normal as he had to travel to where the work was. She was only too aware that her husband was still bitter over Ganya's marriage but how could she have foreseen that he would kill? She explained that he was the family's only bread-winner and therefore she needed him or they might have starved. She was scared of him, but she couldn't see that she had any other choice in life. This same attitude of not rocking the boat prevailed when Ganya became pregnant.

Abortion is illegal in Thailand but there are always means and ways, especially in rural villages. An illegal abortion was easier to deal with and worth the risks involved, than the neighbours finding out what was going on.

I only read up about the case after the execution. It was one of my rules not to research the execution cases until afterwards, preventing me from investing any emotion in the shooting. In Sudjai's case, had I known that he had raped his step-daughter I might have taken pleasure, as a father with a daughter, in killing him which would not be good for my heart or soul. It worked the other way too; I couldn't shoot someone if I doubted their guilt so it was better to know nothing about the circumstances of the person I was to execute. It is beyond my imagination how a grown man could rape a teenager; a 15-year-old is still a child in my eyes and I will never understand men being sexually aroused by children.

Sudjai maintained his innocence and because of the little ambiguities that I referred to earlier he won his case in the Court of Appeal. However, the decision was reversed by the Supreme (or Dika) Court and he was sentenced to death. I imagine that they took the years of raping the girl into consideration and not letting her go, even after she had left to marry because it was a little surprising that he got the death penalty. He only shot Athip once and it was out of jealousy. He didn't try to cut up or hide the body and he had not got a criminal record.

His was my last execution and I thoroughly resented having to do it. I knew that the advent of lethal injection in Bang Kwang was just around the corner, plus it had been a year since the last execution. So I thought I was in the clear, and that shooting people was behind me now. I was very disappointed when I was told to prepare for this one. I had hoped there would be some kind of amnesty, anything that might prevent this shooting from taking place. But nothing happened. I was now beginning to tire of people introducing me to strangers as 'the executioner'. I was also tiring of inappropriate reactions like, 'Hey, so this is what a legal killer looks like!' Did they honestly think I was going to laugh at that?

There was nothing remarkable about my last execution. I didn't speak with the prisoner and there were no scenes of terror or regret from him. For the last time I retrieved the gun and bullets from the armoury. I cleaned them thoroughly and then checked the box of bullets. Each shell had to be inspected for cracks.

When I was satisfied I brought them to my office in the Foreign Affairs Section and locked them into my desk drawer. Then I signed off and headed home, as usual, for a bath and a nap. Tew was the only one who understood how I was feeling; she had also believed that I had executed my last criminal a year ago.

I returned to the prison a couple of hours later and took the guns down to the execution room where I set them up on their stands and waited glumly. I saw Sudjai on my way in when he was getting his photograph and fingerprints taken. His sullen face didn't betray any emotion as he complied with his escorts' directions. Well, that made it a little easier for me. He wrote his will when he was offered a pen and paper and he was either flat broke or really had no feelings for his miserable wife because he wrote in big capital letters that he wished his personal belongings to be left to NO ONE. He arrived at the execution room just after 5pm and was tied to the cross at 5.15pm. At 5.21pm on 11 December 2002 I fired eight bullets, killing him instantly.

***

DOC's Director General Natee Chitsawang, speaking to *The Taipei Times* in 2003, said of the lethal injection that it was a more humane way to execute someone than by firing squad. He even went as far as saying that bringing in this new process might prove to be a stepping stone to abolishing the death penalty altogether. There was a religious ceremony at Bang Kwang when the injection was brought in, officially legalised on 19 October 2003. Monks sprinkled holy water on the machine guns and 319 balloons, representing the spirits of all those shot over the past 71 years, were released. It was hoped that their spirits would go to Heaven. The guns were removed to the museum at the Department of Corrections.

I was very relieved when lethal injection was brought in. It was against my religion to kill another human being, or anything at all. The laymen Buddhist has five commandments to follow: Thou shalt not kill, steal, commit adultery, lie or get drunk. I couldn't really stop after the first execution. There was so a large turnover of Superintendents and all of them would have queried why I was refusing to execute people for them when I had already done it for someone else. I could not afford to lose my job. The farang press constantly asked me why I did it. I had to feed and clothe my family. I was only the last piece in the puzzle that is the Thai justice system. I took the opportunity to end my career as executioner when lethal injection was brought in to replace the gun. Mr Chitsawang agreed, saying that I had done enough over such a long period, so it would be better to stop now. I was glad to be finished with executing. I could now talk about it and write about it. It would not have been appropriate to do so while I was still executioner in case it looked like I was enjoying it. Plus, who would believe me if I spoke about my depression over killing criminals while continuing to do it?

Some prisons in America started using lethal injection back in 1977. Bang Kwang wanted to move with the times. Our forward-thinking chief sent researchers over to America to study the process of injecting a criminal with chemicals. The lower house in the Thai Parliament then voted to bring in lethal injections by 288 to 260. The bill was then supported by the upper house and also received Royal approval. Generally the method was believed to less painful and cruel for the condemned and for the executioner. Death by lethal injection involves three steps. The first is the use of a general anaesthetic, such as sodium pentathol, to relax the prisoner. The second step is the 'paralysing agent', pancuronium bromide, and the third chemical stops the heart, like potassium chloride for instance. A new room was built for the injections, which are activated by three separate buttons to be worked by three separate prison guards, ensuring that one guy does not shoulder the guilt and responsibility.

Just recently I read about China, which executes something like 8,000 people a year. A lot of these executions are performed by firing squads in a public setting—something I would not liked to have done, shooting people in front of a crowd which would probably include the families of the condemned. Anyway, China wants to stop this and have come up with a mobile execution team. A four-man team now picks up a prisoner in a van and drives somewhere quiet to execute him by lethal injection. The Chinese authorities believe this method to be more humane and efficient, and more respectful to the prisoner, instead of making a spectacle out of his death. It is a strange idea.

***

You may find this strange, but when I finished executing prisoners, I decided to enter the priesthood.

It was on the occasion of His Majesty's 72nd birthday which made it even more special. I was 55 years old. Socially every Thai male is expected to become a monk at sometime in his life, just for a short period. Usually you would do so in between finishing school and starting a career and family. It used to be the case that you stayed in the temple for three months during the Buddhist lent season which starts in July alongside the wet season. Thankfully that has been shortened considerably. I didn't experience much enlightenment after my stay of just 15 days. I participated in a mass ordination which included five other prison guards. The Municipal of Nonthaburi organised our entrance into monkhood. I was lucky to join with them since they had all done it before and could show a complete novice like myself the ropes. First I had to shave off my hair and eyebrows. Tew giggled when she saw me. She said it suited me but I'm not so sure.

The other guys had to help me dress the part by getting me into the robes. There are two. First I had to wear a white robe over my shirt and trousers for the initial entrance and then after the preliminary rituals I was presented with the bright orange robe rolled up in a plastic bag. This is the robe that is probably most familiar to tourists. It is a very beautiful garment and a bit complicated to get into. It also took some getting used to, wearing such a vibrant colour. We had to go out walking every morning carrying a large bowl for the offerings that would be presented to us by the public. Thankfully I could wear sandals. The monks used to go out bare foot but then when the roads became dirtier and even treacherous with broken beer bottles etc., they were allowed to put on sandals.

It's not easy being a priest. We had to be up by 4am and showered by 5am every morning. I was glad to return home and catch up on my sleep. When I look at the photos now of me in the orange robe I think I look a bit too self-conscious. I didn't feel truly comfortable as a monk either in the temple or outside on the street but I was glad to do it. It was my way of making merit for my life to date, including being an executioner. I spent the time reading the scriptures and meditating— it was like taking a break to catch my breath from the day to day stressful business of living.

CHAPTER 15

Things are still changing at Bang Kwang. The Department of Corrections is trying to improve its image. Now we only recruit highly-educated staff, people with Bachelor or Masters Degrees. Back when I applied you could be accepted despite not finishing secondary school. The hope is to bring the job of prison guard in line with other civil service careers. The examination and the interview are a lot tougher now than they were. Guards like me are constantly being approached by the rookies who wish to improve their career prospects by writing up projects and proposals for improvements in the prison system. They value our college-free expertise and advice. Old timers like me are becoming fewer and fewer. Yet the rookies can be easily influenced and regularly messed up. Even senior administrative officers are being investigated about corrupt practices—money laundering and supplying drugs.

Working here is a risky business and college degrees are not going to help much if an individual lacks common sense and basic morals. There is too much money involved; money from the prison shop and government money that is allocated to us for improving and extending facilities like the vocational training program. There are plenty of opportunities to be corrupt.

The money from the prison shop is used to buy medicine, and fund events like press receptions when we are trying to get a new program off the ground. There is plenty of money for all of that, but there is precious little for actually feeding the prisoners. Our budget to feed the men remains at 27 baht a day per prisoner. The DOC wants to fix all that now, plus we are working more with international organisations. It is difficult to supply the minimum acceptable standards with such a small budget. I cannot say that the situation has been greatly improved, no matter how highly educated the staff are, or how fancy their surname is.

In the midst of all this change the little things are forgotten about. I know this is not just particular to

Bang Kwang; anyone who has worked at the same job will relate to this. The old guy who has worked hard for years is almost invisible now. These older guys, and I include myself here, were more hands on and got the job done quietly, without fuss. The old guy started his day with a coffee and a smoke at 6am. Then he would have a walk about before unlocking the building. He would ferret out any mishaps from the previous night—who beat up who, who was raped by whom. He always made it his business to know what exactly was going on with the inmates.

He also cared about the little things, like making sure that the inmates got served equal amounts of food. He would watch the inmate who was in charge of dishing out the soup, telling him not to stir it because the meat would be scattered and settle at the bottom of the pot, enabling the convict to dig deep for his mates and skim the meatless surface for everyone else. The server would be instructed to put the fish into the small bowls first and pour the soup over it so that everyone got a bit of meat. The new guys don't concern themselves with any of these voluntary niceties, they don't see the point of them since they haven't been asked by their superiors to carry them out, therefore they won't get any points for it and they won't be paid any extra.

I really don't understand why the DOC hires so many graduates; surely there can't be that many jobs to suit their desired profession. Say we need one good solicitor and we end up taking on ten. That means that nine of them just do errands until they get bored and leave for a better job. The prison is just used as experience to put on a *Curriculum Vitae* and if someone knows that they are not going to be around for a long time then they are reluctant to care about the job. The wages badly need to be improved. A prison officer with a college degree only makes a paltry 7,000 baht a month, which is nothing compared to his counterpart in the business world. The wages are no incentive either to stay or stay away from making dirty money. There would be more pride in the profession if the money was better. The DOC must be careful that all these changes are not purely superficial. The college graduates love proposing new projects. We have boxing tournaments, music competitions and activities galore. But what about the welfare of the prisoners—are they hungry? Are they sick? Is anyone being bullied?

Also I have come to believe that you have to respect the criminals and be a little bit curious about how they arrived in Bang Kwang. It makes the job more bearable and adds to my job satisfaction. If you respect the criminal as an equal human being it pushes you to do your best for him and motivates you to make improvements. Some of the young rookies see the inmates either as guinea pigs for their projects or as errant children. As I have mentioned before, I started to check out their files when they came to the prison and I made it my business to attend a seminar on criminality by the National Council of Thailand. Admittedly, it took me a while to become interested in the criminal as an individual but I'm glad I did. It provided me with a bigger picture and the knowledge that everything is not black and white. When you become a parent you learn it is best to keep an open mind. I think that is why my father was so well-liked—he was always open to new ideas and he was a great believer in the grey areas in life. This is what I have tried to bring to my role in Bang Kwang.

But I also have to repeat what I said earlier. I do believe that some people are innately bad and letting them work in a prison workshop or milk the prison cows is not going to change a serial offender into a good person.

Maintaining self control is a very important social matter in Thailand but it is not always possible. Tourists might find out the hard way that it does not help to lose your temper in public. Thais view a loss of temper to be akin to losing face if you have to resort to shouting and abuse. You are only letting yourself down and making yourself appear inferior. If someone angers you on the street or you feel hard done by you should keep your voice low and smile. This is much more effective behaviour. I could have easily ended up in Bang Kwang myself. When I was younger I was badly beaten up once and I can tell you now that if I had been carrying a gun on me that day I would have been charged for murder or, at the very least, grievous body harm. I was enraged that a gang of men should beat me up for no reason and I was filled with anger and a murderous desire for vengeance. So if it can happen to me it can happen to anyone.

This new breed of prison staff remains oblivious to all that. They sit in their offices hiding behind paperwork and dream up new projects that will enhance their reputations. They send in their projects and continue to sit in their offices waiting to see if they will get a raise for their academic efforts. Meanwhile I have befriended the inmate who cleans my office in the mornings. He fills me in on all the goings-on in the wings. If someone has been beaten up, I ask to see the head of the cell where the beating took place. I ask him what happened and after further investigation on my part I transfer the victim to another cell if I don't think he is going to be left in peace. This is how I have always operated.

Now, I don't really have anything against these projects. They help the prison, which can only be a positive thing. My problem is that when one guy starts doing a project and receives praise for it, then the others follow suit and there is no actual prison officer work being done. The new guys decide that a sport exhibition should be put in place. They hand out surveys and questionnaires and work out their statistics and percentages. The older warden worries about whether one prisoner will use the dumbbells to knock out a guy he doesn't like, or the guy who has flirted with his 'ladyboy', or even a guard he has had a run-in with. He wonders where the prisoners are going to have their work out in relation to what the other prisoners are doing. Where is the equipment going to be left? Who is going to mind the key? The older guys have a lot more questions while the newer guys just present answers to questions that haven't been asked.

Everything changes and I shouldn't really be complaining. The world is changing. During one riot the inmates flew a kite to ask for Royal Amnesty. Today they use mobile phones.

***

People ask me if I believe in the prison system, do I believe that Bang Kwang can receive a hardened criminal and make him a better person to send back to live in normal society? I would have to be honest and say that I'm not sure that Bang Kwang has ever, or could ever, achieve that. There is a man from the Middle East who comes here looking to counsel the prisoners in the hope that he will make a few converts. In fact the prison receives quite a few religious teachers. They probably have the best of intentions and take the time to ask the prisoners what it is they are really looking for; how do they think faith could be introduced into their lives to help them. I maintain that all an inmate ever wants is his freedom; he's not too hung up about improving his health or mind, he just wants to go home.

In my opinion there are three kinds of prisoners. The first kind is the 'born-to-be' criminal. He is like a lotus that lives under water and shies away from the light. I remember having a conversation with a serial rapist. He talked about not having the patience to befriend a woman and make the effort to get to know her over a few months before she lets him into her bed. He preferred the short cut. This is not easy talk to listen to, especially as a father and husband. I tried to explain that waiting and working towards something would lead to a more enduring satisfaction, one that lasted longer than three minutes, and would leave him feeling like he had really accomplished something. But I couldn't be sure that he really understood what I was saying.

The second kind is the easily influenced criminal who finds himself in trouble thanks to his brother or his gang; he just went with the flow without aim or ambition.

The third kind is the mentally challenged criminal. He ends up in jail through a lack of intelligence or abnormal social skills. The first and the third criminal have, more than likely, had a crap childhood riddled with neglect or abuse—sexual or violent. They all end up here, after damaging someone else, needing to be rehabilitated and healed. We are not very optimistic regarding their leaving Bang Kwang as completely different people.

It is too heavy a responsibility to place that huge burden on the Department of Corrections alone;

society at large also has to change its attitude. What is the point of bringing a prisoner into the workshop here and providing him with a skill? Maybe we can train an inmate to be a great carpenter or a cook but then he gets released into the outside world with his new found skill and when he turns up for a job interview with a prison record nobody wants to take a chance and hire him. So he ends up broke and completely vulnerable to resuming whatever it was he was doing that got him thrown into Bang Kwang in the first place. The politicians don't seem too interested in the problems of the DOC, which is a pity because we should all be working together. The DOC is like the child of a mistress; no one wants to support us or give us a bigger budget.

We do our best here in the prison. The prisoners have access to sport, a choir, religion as well as the vocational training. We also have a prison house band, made up of inmates, and even our very own DJ, who used to work for a Thai country music radio station before being charged with drug offences. He runs a radio station from the auditorium which the band sometimes plays in. We used to hold quite a few concerts in the auditorium; I even played there a couple of times over the years. Unfortunately we have mostly stopped inviting musicians to the prison after the 1985 riot. The best concert I ever saw in Bang Kwang was actually a comedy show that was put on by the famous Thai comedienne Noi Po-ngam. She and her friends just cracked me up. Nowadays a show might be put on for a special occasion but that's about it.

We have to function according to the standards and requirements set by the humanitarian organisations that Bang Kwang has joined. Overall the life of a prisoner has improved a lot since I started working as a prison guard. If a prisoner feels that he is being treated badly by a guard he is free to lodge a complaint against that guard. This was completely unheard of in the olden days. Things are better for the prisoner but this means extra work for the officer. Even the language has changed; we should call them inmates and not prisoners, while we are officers and not prison guards. As if that makes a difference!

***

Whether Bang Kwang has the ability to furnish a man with morals, if his parents and teachers have failed him, is open to debate. At the end of the day I believe that every human has his own value and I think I can honestly say that I have never looked down on any inmate. I don't believe in kicking a man when he's down, but on the other hand I'm not ready to believe that we can make them into better people. All we can do is send them back into society after they have completed their sentence and hope that they won't commit the same crime again. They are lucky to receive a second opportunity. Yes we should think positively, but we don't want to be accused of naivety either.

For my part in the prison system all I can do is control them and prevent them from escaping, and ensure they are equipped with the essentials for living here. The inmates want officers to understand how bad their position is, and we do understand, more so than anyone else on the planet. If I think a prisoner isn't a truly bad person I would befriend him but not completely trust him. I have to be realistic. I might find he has a common interest in music. Prisoners are always surprised to see me playing the guitar or hear me talk about Elvis or the music scene in the 1970s. Equally if an inmate is upset because his wife hasn't visited him in a long time I would fetch him pen and paper so that he could write to her. If I had any stamps in my wallet I would take his letter and post it for him on my way home. I wouldn't contact the family directly which, as

I have said before, is a violation of prison rules. If you want to try and improve someone you must win him over first.

***

I am now the head of the Foreign Affairs Section in the prison and have been for the last six years. There are around 10,000 foreign criminals in Thailand now, so you can appreciate the necessity of this section. One of my biggest responsibilities is to organise the visits for the foreign relatives who fly in to see their loved one. There are constantly mountains of complaints from these prisoners requiring my attention. There are literally thousands of letters that have to be inspected and filed away and they are in a variety of languages; English, Chinese, French and Hindi, and it can be quite difficult staying on top of it. It used to be a much slower process, in that each letter from a foreign convict had to be first sent to the Department of Corrections where it might lie about for months before it was sent back to us. Thankfully we don't have to do that anymore. But still the letters do mount up. Some embassies, like Israel, kindly help us by confirming what the letters sent by their convicts are about.

Even if all the different nationalities spoke English badly, most Thai prison guards do not speak English. They tend to just say shake their head to whatever they are being asked and wave the prisoner away. Therefore the foreign inmate does not feel that he is being looked after or that he had the same rights as the other prisoners. We have to able to answer their questions. One guy got very frustrated in his efforts to obtain permission to marry his girlfriend in prison. In fact I have had to help obtain several marriage licenses by now, which is a pleasant matter to be involved in but is a real bitch, paperwork-wise. As always I take my role very seriously and work hard at it. Sometimes the complaints are a little silly like the few times I have been asked why their relatives haven't written to them. I would love to simply reply with another question, like, 'How the hell would I know?' Instead I suggest that the prisoner tells his family to either send their letters through their embassy or register their letters so that the post office can track them—if these letters actually exist in the first place.

We even provide internet access for the prisoners which I am delighted with. If the prisoner prefers he can write a letter and we can scan it for him and email it. When the reply comes through we print it out and give it to him. This service is also available for Thai convicts but they largely prefer contact visits from their families to letters and emails. It is prison policy that each prisoner is entitled to a voice and communicate any complaints he may have.

I also have to deal with complaints about heath matters and insufficient treatments. Mostly the convicts send their complaints first to their embassies or NGO (Non Government Organisation) who then passes on the query or complaint to the Superintendent here, asking him to do something about it. We would then send a letter to the Director of the local hospital asking for a doctor to attend to the prisoner to see how serious the case is. Sometimes the prisoner specifies which hospital he wants to be treated in and the attending doctor must confirm that his illness cannot be treated successfully by the prison clinic. The prisoner must also be made to understand that he will have to pay for all his medical expenses. The prison does provide a limited amount of medicine free of charge but certainly something like a hospital stay has to be covered by the inmate himself.

The most years that a foreign prisoner spends with us is eight, before either being released or being transferred to his own country for further imprisonment. These are the hard core cases, like drug-selling. For lesser crimes it is between two and three years. We have different transfer agreements with 44 countries. There is a committee made up of officials from the Justice Ministry and the individual embassy that look after each transfer case. The embassy sends us a request regarding a prisoner and we send them back the details of the crime committed and the sentence handed down. We also send the photographs and fingerprints and everything is stamped by me to confirm that the prisoner is eligible for transfer. The embassy then has a meeting to discuss said prisoner. If everything is fine they request another pack of the same documents from us. Then the embassy confers with the Department of Corrections.

Obviously the most important part of my job is to make sure that the right prisoner is transferred. Fortunately I have never sent the wrong guy packing but what did happen was that a guy was almost on the plane before it was realised that he hadn't actually finished his sentence. The police had filed another charge against him but a warrant hadn't been issued yet. They had to ask a judge to specially set a hearing and issue a verdict on the same day in order to allow his transfer to continue.

I have to say that the American team probably impresses me the most with their efficiency and organisational skills. Two days before the transfer of an American national, and without any nagging on my part, the Ambassador, embassy officials, prosecutor and police will arrive at Bang Kwang to visit the prisoner to read him his rights so that he knows exactly what is going on. Each transfer is presided over by our Superintendent, and because I head the Foreign Affair Section I am always a witness. I don't play any part in the escorting of the prisoner to the airport, except for one time when we transferred almost 100 Nigerians and extra officers were required to accompany them. An entire plane had been booked for them. Needless to say there was a lot of paperwork that day. Immigration officers had to come out to Bang Kwang to go through all the documents and passports before the men could leave the prison.

It is very hard work, but I also enjoy it as there is a big social aspect to this position. I have a drawer crammed with all the little gifts that I have received from foreign officials, from an 'I Love New York' key-ring to a badge of the Canadian flag. My favourite is probably the head of the Statue of Liberty on a chain, or maybe the FBI badge. The embassies are particularly generous around Christmas and New Year and I receive many cards and bottles of wine. I was never one to say no to a party and get invited to many functions now at all the embassies. The Superintendent and I are the only two ever invited from Bang Kwang and I go to every single one of them. Sometimes he allows me to use prison money to bring flowers or a fruit basket along.

I must have a passion for collecting things as I have kept every party invite I have ever received. I receive regular invites from the Canadian, English, American, Malaysian and Singaporean embassies. Some of them make me laugh as the spelling of my names varies drastically from embassy to embassy.

They are not very wild parties—quite unlike the ones on the American military bases when I was a teenaged musician. They usually start about 6.30pm and finish up just two hours later. The location can be the Ambassador's residence or somewhere equally plush like the five star Shangri-la or Hyatt Erawan Hotel. I never really enjoy the food—the bite-size finger food usually leaves me hungrier after I have eaten it. However, I always enjoy tasting the different wines and being introduced to the other guests. I have always enjoyed meeting new people so this job suits me very well.

Sometimes it comes in very handy, like the time when my daughter worked briefly for a photography studio run by a Taiwanese man who didn't pay her as promised. I got on the phone to Chan, the Director of the Thai-Taiwan Business Association, who I had met at a party. He asked me for the studio's phone number and a little while later my daughter received her wages. One of my favourite officials is Kate from the British Embassy. She once looked after me at a party and made sure to introduce me to everyone present. I knew her for a while because she is the one who contacts me about matters relating to the British inmates. I like her because she respects the Thai officers and is a good listener. You can have a proper discussion with her and so properly explain why you can or cannot help with a specific request.

***

In the bigger picture I hope to be able to make a positive contribution to the Thai penal system. I collect as much information as I can so that I can present a history detailing the developments, the turning points and so on. Perhaps in ten years time there will be no death penalty, it will just be found in the history books or in the Museum belonging to the Department of Corrections where I help out as a guide at least once a month and lecture on the different stages of execution in Thailand, from beheading to firing squad to lethal injection. The government might decide that it has no right to take the life of a man no matter what he has done, because it is not a low life criminal, it is the government. Therefore, executing people should not be something that it condones. I have come to believe that severe punishment does nothing to solve the problem of crime but it should function as an extreme warning. I best describe it like this: You are two years old and you try to cross a busy street by yourself, almost ending up under the wheels of a car. Your mother grabs you in horror and slaps you several times to scare you from ever doing that again. There has to be consequences for committing a crime and there has to be deterrents—particularly for the ones who stop to think about what they are doing, or stop to plan a cold-blooded murder or rape.

***

And now for the question that I am asked the most— do I regret being an executioner? I have given this a lot of thought and have even discussed it with Buddhist monks. Their opinion is usually the same; the convicts on death row are swamped in bad karma and the executioner is doing them a favour by sending them on to their next incarnation for the chance to redeem themselves.

Things used to be a hell of a lot worse for convicts in Thailand. A long, long time ago a convict's chest would have been ripped open to see if his heart was any different from that of a normal person and his skull would have been split open for the same reason, to look at his brain. I should mention that the convict was usually alive when this was happening. After his head had been chopped off it was jammed on to a long stick which was then put up in a public place as an example to anyone who was planning on committing devious deeds. I am quite sure that the Western world could also offer many examples of man's inhumanity to man, then and now.

I believe in karma, which can be bad or good depending on the individual. I never got any pleasure out of shooting people, or out of performing any other role in the execution process. It was my job. Did the World War Two pilot who dropped bombs create bad karma for himself? Or what about the American solders in Iraq? Should they be blamed for atrocities committed instead of the man responsible for sending them out there in the first place? Killing criminals troubled and depressed me. I always felt truly sorry for the condemned and things like Ginggaew's prolonged dying will never leave me. It depressed all of us involved. Nobody looked forward to an execution. It was a duty to be carried out, and as such I wanted to do it to the best of my ability. You only create bad karma if your intention was bad. If I had enjoyed the killing I would be worried now, but my conscience is clear.

Killing wasn't easy. Generally speaking when we talk about jobs we are talking about something productive. Everyone likes to be proud of what they do for a living but obviously I couldn't. During my years of execution some of the superior officers looked down on me. They assumed that I was full of ego because of what I did so they didn't wish to add to my 'arrogance' by treating me in a civilised manner. I also use to sense awkwardness at parties that Tew and I attended. I could feel people catch one another eyes and gesture in my direction. People didn't want to socialise with me because, like my father, they believed all prison guards to be stupid and brutal. However, I also saw an opportunity to change people's view of executioners and therefore of all prison guards.

I'm an unusual executioner in that I'm westernised to a certain degree; I play the guitar and I enjoy attending parties. If people were expecting to see a mad man thirsting for blood and brandishing a sword, then they were disappointed. If they were expecting me to spew forth hatred for criminals and their doings they were disappointed. I didn't want their fear. I was an ordinary man whose biggest priority has always been my family. I never forget who or what I represent. The ones closest to me understood how tough I found the job and they were all I cared about.

My oldest son would complain over the years when his friends clamoured to be invited to the family home in order to see me, the executioner, in the flesh. Luckily he is a grounded kid and would huffily explain that 'executioner' wasn't my title or who I was, only a duty that I had to do infrequently.

Then I found myself becoming a minor celebrity. Journalists, Thai and foreign, have sought me out to ask me about my job and Bang Kwang. One of Thai TV's biggest personalities, Sawrayuth, understood my position immediately, which I really appreciated. He saw the job of executioner as being completely unwanted, depressing and thankless. He also said that he couldn't understand how I managed to do it for so long. Students approached me for help on their thesis' concerning the penal system. That still happens today and I'm always happy to oblige. If they are especially lucky I will bring them back to my house and Tew will cook them a meal. What I don't appreciate are the thrill seekers, the ones who just want the bloodiest and goriest details. They seem to think that I enjoyed it too.

I even speak at universities to warn young people about the temptations that lie beyond the college campus. My father would have been proud of me for this—I think he would have liked me to have gone into teaching. It is unrealistic just to tell young people to say no to crime and spin them fairy tales about good and bad witches. You must arm them with knowledge and information about the many ways it is possible to break the law. My tales are full of blood and gore but it gets my point across much more effectively. I tried to make something good out of my years of executing people by talking about how bad things can get if you are arrested and sentenced to Bang Kwang. If I can save even some of my young listeners and persuade them against committing a crime, then it is well worth it. The kids always ask me how many people I have 'killed'—not executed—or if I could execute a relative, which proves that they are only concentrating so much on my warnings against breaking the law!

Tew always supported me no matter what I did but I knew that she looked forward to the day when I was no longer executioner. I know she used to wonder why I didn't push myself forward and try to ingratiate myself with my superiors but that was just out of loyalty to me. She always wished I was appreciated more and paid even more than that. I watched other men do it over the years—get involved with the office politics in order to get themselves ahead. Although to be honest it's an expensive business, undertaking to keep a boss supplied in whiskey or his favourite tobacco. It might take years before it paid off. I did buy presents maybe once a year around New Year's Eve which is normal Thai practice but some of the men would decide to lick ass big time and end up spending a fortune. Some of the more well-to-do would buy presents for the boss's family. I found it entertaining. There was a lot of string pulling, especially in the earlier days. The Thai official system was very rooted in a patronage system. Who you knew or who you were related to was most important.

***

Tew and I are together 40 years now, which was a lot of hard work on our part. She will say that she never experienced any difficulties when I was executing people. The neighbours all knew what I did and accepted it. In truth I don't think she rushed to tell a stranger about what her husband did for a living. We have had a good life together and enjoy attending parties and socialising more than ever. Our biggest rows mostly took place when the kids were younger. Every couple's relationship has an Achilles Heel. When I disciplined the kids Tew would sometimes want to throw in a few slaps where I felt a couple of stern words would suffice. Then the children would be forgotten as she went storming off in tears and I would be left feeling angry and guilty.

Unlike some of my friends I was lucky to have a wife who never attempted to assault me or call me names no matter how mad she got. I would not have liked a dragon for a wife; I do not see the attraction of hot-headed aggressive women. I just prefer a quiet life as much as possible. I think the secret to a good marriage lies in establishing a good friendship with your spouse.

If a prisoner boasted to me about beating up his wife or insulting her in front of his mates I would ask him if he could treat a friend like that, and the answer was always, 'No way!'

We are both immensely proud of our three children; we worked hard to ensure they received the best education that we could afford. I believe it is best to provide a child with as many choices as possible, and the sense to make an informed decision. And now we are grandparents and a new generation has begun again.

When I first started with the prison we were given a small one storey wooden house nearby that used to be a barber shop. It was handy for work but the neighbourhood wasn't great. It was bearable for the first while but the older my kids got the unhappier I became. I guess it reminded me of where I grew up and I just wanted something better for my family. Many of the prison officers also lived in the area and they would drink heavily after work so there was a lot of drunkenness. Some of their wives were a common lot and they would sit around playing cards or talking inappropriately in front of the children. Teenage pregnancy was prevalent, as if there was nothing else to do. These people had given up hope and just lived the lives of their impoverished parents.

I didn't want my kids picking up wanton habits like smoking, drinking and casual sex. They had to learn that there was a better way of living. I became determined that they get the best education that I could afford. It took a few years of hard saving for Tew and I but we eventually were able to move to another town house in the mid-1980s. We have been rewarded tenfold for our efforts; all my kids are doing really well and are completely independent of their parents, which means we have done our job properly.

I have always been interested in politics, have even considered going into local politics, and make sure I keep up with news and events. If I did get involved I would concentrate on crime prevention, especially regarding young people. Crime prevention should begin within the small communities, making sure that our young people are aware of all the pitfalls that can befall them. Thailand doesn't only attract thousands of tourists, but also thousands of foreign criminals. Young people should be well educated against manipulation to sell or courier drugs, as well as taking them. The police receive a cash bonus when they bust a drug case so they go out looking for naïve people who are in need of money. If someone tells you that they know how you could make some easy money, it could be a police officer waiting to trap you. Anyway it is just something I am thinking about for the moment.

***

My mother is still alive. We have kept in touch more frequently since my father's death. She is well into her 80s and has suffered a stroke and a bad fall. Tew and I visit her as much as we can but I think she is closer to my brother Oud. He has worked harder than me at building a relationship with her. Oud just retired recently from his job as prison officer at Kong Prem prison. We see each other pretty regularly. She enjoys my kids, especially my second son who knows how to charm her and make her laugh.

I no longer play the guitar for weddings or parties but I still play it to relax me and when I am coerced at family gatherings. My taste in music hasn't changed much since the 60s. I still revere Elvis, Cliff Richard and The Beatles. Over the years I added the Bee Gees to my prolific music collection. Tew constantly moans about dusting my records, CDs and now MP3 CDs. My favourite song to perform on the guitar has to be The

Beatles' 'Yesterday'. I enjoy going to the cinema twice a month with my daughter. It is nice to spend some time with her and keep abreast of the latest movies, even though I remain unconvinced that they are better than the likes of *Ben Hur* or *The Ten Commandments*. Charlton Heston was always a particular favourite of mine. Having said that, I have to confess to loving *Narnia* and the *Lord of The Rings* trilogy!

I have also developed a passion for history and when I can I love to settle into my favourite chair with a beer or a glass of wine and eat up political biographies from the likes of Gandhi and the Kennedy dynasty, as well as important Thais like Preedee Panomyong. I also enjoy reading about the key moments in the history of Thailand like why and how the special execution orders came about, and how Thailand moved from a monarchy to a democracy in 1932. Maybe I am a frustrated academic after all! I just want to keep my brain and mind active, there is always something new to learn.

I don't fret about getting older and I am not afraid of dying. I don't know if that has anything to do with my career path. Death is inevitable. If I have a terminal disease I wouldn't bother with any doctors. I wouldn't allow my kids to spend money on trying to prolong my life. I have seen stricken families take out loans and sell their properties in order to be able to spend more money on medical care for an obviously dying relative. That will not happen to me. The thing is to die happy and not to leave any trouble behind for your spouse or kids to deal with. I have everything sorted and ready—I am a practical man.

***

I am grateful to Bang Kwang for many things. It enabled me to educate my children and it changed the way that I looked at the world. I used to be the sort of person who sees an angry elephant instead of just a little ant but I have calmed down considerably. I have seen some terrible things which helped me to better appreciate the good things in my life, big and small. There is always light in darkness and none of us are here forever. This is my last personal duty to conclude, my own little book of which I am immensely proud. The years of keeping diaries and developing the practice of noting daily what I saw has finally paid off.

My name is Chavoret Jaruboon. I was born into a broken family. My home was a stone's throw away from a brothel and the smell of opium was heavy in the air when I walked to school each morning. I could easily have become a drug addict or an alcoholic.

Instead, I learned how to play the guitar, listened to those wiser than me, and worked hard to give my family a better life. I could never have known, when I first took to the stage with my band, that I would be swept along with life's changes and would become the figure I was at the 'Bangkok Hilton', that is, the man at Bang Kwang prison who would end the lives of 55 men and women; the last executioner.

WELCOMETOHELL

ONE MAN'S FIGHT FOR LIFE INSIDE THE BANGKOK HILTON
by Colin Martin

Written from his cell and smuggled out page by page, Colin Martin's autobiography chronicles an innocent man's struggle to survive inside one of the world's most dangerous prisons.

After being swindled out of a fortune, Martin was let down by the hopelessly corrupt Thai police. Forced to rely upon his own resources, he tracked down the man who conned him and, drawn into a fight, accidentally stabbed and killed that man's bodyguard.

Martin was arrested, denied a fair trial, convicted of murder and thrown into prison—where he remained for eight years.

Honest and often disturbing—but told with a surprising humour—Welcome to Hell is the remarkable story of how Martin was denied justice again and again.

In his extraordinary account, he describes the swindle, his arrest and vicious torture by police, the unfair trial, andthe eight years of brutality and squalor he was forced to endure.

To order this book go to www.maverickhouse.com

YOU'LL NEVER WALK ALONE

A TRUE STORY ABOUT THE BANGKOK HILTON

by Debbie Singh

Debbie Singh's life fell apart when she received a letter from her brother out of the blue. He had been sentenced to ten years in Klong Prem prison, the notorious 'Bangkok Hilton', for fencing a $1000 cheque.

The severity of the sentence shocked Singh, and she immediately set off to Bangkok to visit him, offer her support, and locate his Thai-born son.

Appalled by the horrendous circumstances she found
him in, she started a campaign to have him transferred to an Australian jail, something never achieved before. This campaign changed her life - and that of her family - forever.

With great honesty and heart, You'll Never Walk Alone tells the story of Singh's great determination and strength in the face of adversity, the rollercoaster ride of emotions she had to face in the six year struggle to save her brother, her ongoing charity work, and the heartbreak she felt as her life was torn apart by a bitter twist in the tale.

To order this book go to www.maverickhouse.com

HEROIN

A TRUE STORY OF DRUG ADDICTION, HOPE AND TRIUMPH
By Julie O'Toole

Heroin is a story of hope; a story of a young woman's emergence from the depths of drug addiction and despair.

Julie O'Toole started using heroin in her mid-teens. A bright young girl, she quickly developed a chronic addiction and her life spiralled out of control. Enslaved to the drug, Julie began shoplifting to feed her habit before offering to work as a drug dealer for notorious gangsters.

Julie was eventually saved by the care and support of a drugs counsellor, and by her own strength to endure.

Heroin is a tale of how a young girl became a victim of circumstances.

Julie's story takes us from Dublin's inner city to London and America, and gives an insight into how anyone can become a victim of circumstances.

With honesty and insight, Julie tells of the horror and degradation that came with life as a drug addict, and reveals the extraordinary strength of will that enabled her to conquer heroin addiction and to help others do the same.

NIGHTMARE IN LAOS

by Kay Danes

Hours after her husband Kerry was kidnapped by the Communist Laos government, Kay Danes tried to flee to Thailand with her two youngest children, only to be intercepted at the border.

Torn away from them and sent to an undisclosed location, it was then that the nightmare really began. Forced to endure 10 months of outrageous injustice and corruption, she and her husband fought for their freedom from behind the filth and squalor of one of Laos' secret gulags.

Battling against a corrupt regime, she came to realise that there were many worse off people held captive in Laos—people without a voice, or any hope of freedom.

Kay had to draw from the strength and spirit of those around her in order to survive this hidden hell, while the world media and Australian government tried desperately to have her and Kerry freed before it was too late and all hope was lost.

For Kay, the sorrow and pain she saw people suffer at the hands of the regime in Laos, where human rights are non-existent, will stay with her forever, and she vowed to tell the world what she has seen. This is her remarkable story.

To order this book go to www.maverickhouse.com